L I P I D S

in

P R I M A R Y

C A R E

LIPIDS
in
PRIMARY CARE

Dr Paul M Dodson MD FRCP FRCOphth
Professor Anthony H Barnett BSc MD FRCP

Department of Medicine and Diabetes,
Birmingham Heartlands Hospital,
Birmingham, UK

THE MEDICAL PUBLISHING
company

Publisher: *The Medical Publishing Company*
40–42 Osnaburgh Street, London NW1 3ND

Project management: *Richard Yarwood*
Carol Mason
Design: *Steve Lampon*

ISBN 0 9533278 0 9

British Library Cataloguing in Publication Data.
A catalogue record is available from the British Library.

Printed in The United Kingdom by Fisherprint Ltd, Peterborough

PREFACE

It was established over 20 years ago that high plasma cholesterol is one of the most important causal risk factors for coronary heart disease (CHD). Absolute evidence that cholesterol-lowering reduces cardiovascular events and overall mortality, however, has only recently become available. Recent trials have emphasized the importance of lipid-lowering in both the prevention and the treatment of CHD. Although plasma cholesterol and low density lipoprotein-cholesterol (LDL-cholesterol) play an important part in the development of atherosclerosis, it is now clear that other lipid abnormalities, including low levels of high density lipoprotein-cholesterol (HDL-cholesterol) and elevated triglyceride, are involved in the disease process.

In the 1980s, there was a reluctance to treat lipid abnormalities from the point of view of primary or secondary prevention, since although the intervention trials had demonstrated a reduction in CHD events, they had not influenced total mortality. It was therefore argued that drug therapy for treatment of lipid disorders should be reserved only for those patients with major lipid abnormalities. The 1990s, however, have seen the introduction of newer and safer lipid-lowering drugs, the statins, and trials have shown that these drugs have a major impact on the cardiovascular events and total mortality. The major intervention trials have now changed clinical debate from whether lipid-lowering is effective to whether we can afford the cost of widespread prescription for lipid disorders!

The first chapters of this book are a guide through the complexities of lipid structure and metabolism, and their relationship to CHD. This is followed by a discussion of the clinical features and definitions of the hyperlipidaemias, the results from the most recent lipid-lowering trials and the strategies for treatment. The book is written by practising clinicians with a major clinical and research interest in this subject area. We have tried to provide a readable and logical format to aid understanding of lipid disorders and of the importance of appropriate clinical management.

Dr Paul M Dodson
Professor Anthony H Barnett

THE AUTHORS

In 1974 Paul M Dodson MD FRCP FRCOphth qualified at St. Bartholomew's Hospital, London. His early years were spent training at Southampton General Hospital and the Royal Berkshire Hospital in Reading. In 1979 he returned to St Bartholomew's and Moorfields Eye Hospital, London to conduct research into hyperlipidaemias and retinopathy. This led to his MD. In 1982 he moved to Dudley Road Hospital, Birmingham to undertake the position of Senior Registrar in Endocrinology. By 1989 he had been appointed Consultant Physician in Medicine, Diabetes and Endocrinology at Birmingham Heartlands Hospital. Currently his research interests include: medical ophthalmology (diabetic retinopathy and retinovascular disease), diabetes mellitus, hypertension and hyperlipidaemia.

Anthony H Barnett BSc (Hons) MD FRCP qualified in medicine at King's College Hospital, London in 1975. This followed a first class honours degree in pharmacology obtained in 1972. His early years of training were spent at King's College Hospital, Coventry and then Leeds before finally returning to King's in 1978 to undertake the position of Clinical Registrar in diabetic medicine. Between 1979 and 1981 he undertook a post as Medical Research Council Senior Fellow in the same unit. Subsequent to the successful completion of his MD, he continued his training as a Senior Registrar in New Zealand and Southampton. In 1983 he was appointed Senior Lecturer in Medicine and Diabetes and Honorary Consultant Physician at the University of Birmingham and Birmingham Heartlands Hospital. Promotion to a Reader in Medicine followed in 1989 and finally to Professor of Medicine in 1992. His current research interests include the genetics of diabetes, susceptibility factors for microvascular complications and therapeutic interventions, with a particular interest in susceptibility factors for diabetic nephropathy, its prevention and treatment.

Previously the authors have published several books in areas such as diabetes, the genetics of diabetes, hyperlipidaemia, hypertension, retinopathies, and nutrition and cholesterol reduction.

Contents

1. **Lipids and lipoprotein metabolism**   1

    Structure of lipids 1
    Lipids in the circulation 2
    Lipid metabolism 5
        - introduction 5
        - the exogenous pathways 5
        - the endogenous pathways 6
        - reverse cholesterol transport 8
        - the LDL receptor 8
        - the enterohepatic circulation 9

2. **Major lipid risk factors in coronary heart disease**   10

    Atheroma formation 10
    Risk factors for coronary heart disease 14
    Cholesterol and coronary heart disease 15
    Triglyceride and HDL in coronary heart disease 16
    Non-lipid risk factors and coronary heart disease 17

3. **Hyperlipidaemia**   20

    What lipid levels are normal? 20
    Clinical classification of hyperlipidaemias 21
        - primary hyperlipidaemias 22
        - secondary hyperlipidaemias 24
    Clinical features of hyperlipidaemias 24

4. **Lipid lowering and reduction of coronary heart disease risk**   29

    Why treat lipid disorders? 29
    Does treating lipid disorders reduce atherosclerosis? ... 29
    Intervention trials 31

CONTENTS

5. Strategy for lipid-screening and   37
   management of hyperlipidaemia

Introduction 37
Screening strategies 38
    - population screening 38
    - targeted screening approach 39
    - who should be screened? 39
    - how should lipids be measured? 40
    - assessment of risk 41
Diagnosis of hyperlipidaemia 46
Management of hyperlipidaemia 47
    - non-pharmacological management 50
    - drug therapy for the treatment of hyperlipidaemia 52
    - statins (3-hydroxy 3-methylglutaryl-CoA 53
      reductase inhibitors)
    - fibrates 56
    - resins 57
    - nicotinic acid compounds 57
    - fish oils 58
    - probucol 58
    - drug combinations 58
    - management strategies 59
    - acute severe combined hyperlipidaemia 62
    - other therapies for refractory hyperlipidaemia 62
    - key issues in the management of lipid disorders 63

6. Further reading   65

Chapter one 65
Chapter two 65
Chapter three 66
Chapter four 67
Chapter five 68

7. Index   71

LIPIDS AND LIPOPROTEIN METABOLISM

Structure of lipids

Lipids are a heterogeneous group of compounds that have in common the property of solubility in organic solvents and insolubility in water. The major lipid components of importance in human metabolism are cholesterol, triglycerides and phospholipids. Cholesterol has a four-ringed structure (Figure 1.1) and triglycerides are formed from a three carbon glycerol molecule to which fatty acid side chains are joined by ester linkages (Figure 1.2). Phospholipids are similar to triglycerides, except that in phospholipids one fatty acid is replaced by a phosphate-containing group. Fatty acids may also be joined to cholesterol-producing cholesterol esters which constitute the majority of circulating cholesterol with 25% remaining 'free', and not joined to fatty acids.

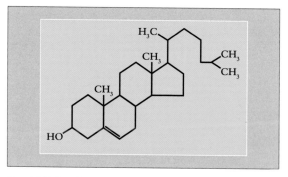

Figure 1.1 **Cholesterol structure.**

Fatty acids consist of chains of carbon atoms with an acid group (—COOH) at one end. If the carbon atoms are all joined by single bonds the structure is referred to as 'saturated' due to its high melting point. The introduction of a double bond into the fatty acid structure results in monosaturation and multiple double bonds lead to the more

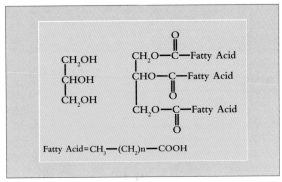

Figure 1.2 Structure of glycerol (left) and triglycerides (right).

open structure of polyunsaturated fatty acids. When glycerol is esterified with fatty acids the non-polar triglycerides are formed. They are stored in adipose tissue and represent an energy source from which fatty acids can be released. Phospholipid molecules are formed from the esterification of glycerol with phosphate-containing molecules. These phospholipid molecules and cholesterol are the major components of cell membranes. Cholesterol is the precursor of a number of steroid hormones and is converted to bile acids.

When energy is required, triglycerides in adipose tissue are hydrolysed to release fatty acids. Free fatty acids then undergo a series of reactions which release energy.

Lipids in the circulation

Lipid measurements in blood usually include cholesterol and triglycerides. These molecules are insoluble in water and therefore have to be complexed with certain proteins in order to become water soluble and transported in plasma. These proteins are apolipoproteins and in combination with triglyceride, cholesterol, cholesterol ester and phospholipid, they form large complex structures known as lipoproteins. In the lipoprotein structures, the polar head of each phospholipid group projects from the surface of the particle into the aqueous environment, whereas the non-polar portions project into the core of the particle (Figure 1.3).

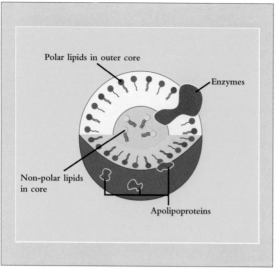

Figure 1.3 Lipoprotein structure.

Lipoprotein	Major lipid component	Size (nm diameter)
Chylomicrons	Triglyceride	500
Very low density lipoprotein	Triglyceride	43
Intermediate density lipoprotein	Cholesterol/triglyceride	27
Low density lipoprotein	Cholesterol	22
High density lipoprotein	Cholesterol	8

Table 1.1 Classification of lipoproteins.

The lipoprotein particles can be separated according to their density using ultracentrifugation. The particles with relatively more lipid are less dense and those with more apolipoprotein are more dense. Lipoprotein classes with their size are shown in Table 1.1. The largest but least dense are the chylomicrons, which are normally only present in the postprandial state and are triglyceride rich. Cholesterol and its esters are more dense than triglycerides and are therefore present in a greater proportion as the density of the particle increases. The main cholesterol-carrying lipoprotein is low-density lipoprotein (LDL)-cholesterol, comprising approximately 70% of the total plasma cholesterol; high-density lipoprotein (HDL) accounts for 20% of the total plasma cholesterol. Both of these lipoprotein classes are heterogeneous in composition. HDL can be fractioned into two major subfractions, HDL2 and HDL3. Similarly, LDL-cholesterol has three sub-fractions with LDL3 being the smallest and most dense particle. The main triglyceride-carrying lipoproteins are chylomicrons and VLDL (very low-density lipoprotein). VLDL accounts for approximately 60% of total plasma cholesterol in the fasting state.

Apolipoprotein	Lipoprotein
A-I,II	HDL
B-48	Chylomicron remnants
B-100	VLDL, IDL, LDL
C-II, C-III	Chylomicrons, VLDL
E	VLDL, IDL, HDL

HDL = High density lipoprotein
VLDL = Very low-density lipoprotein
IDL = Intermediate density lipoprotein
LDL = Low density lipoprotein

Table 1.2 **Major classes of apolipoproteins.**

Apolipoproteins are key structures in the synthesis and secretion of lipoproteins from the liver or intestine (Table 1.2). They play a dynamic role in lipoprotein metabolism as enzyme activators and receptor ligands. The major apolipoprotein of LDL and VLDL is apolipoprotein B-100 (apo B-100), whereas apolipoprotein E (apo E) is the binding ligand for chylomicron remnants, with the apo E receptor situated in the liver. The significance of these apolipoproteins is that the LDL receptor binds those lipoproteins that contain apo B-100 and/or apo E. Receptors in the liver recognise apo E and bind chylomicron remnants. Abnormalities in these receptors or in the apolipoprotein mean that there is no longer complete recognition, resulting in a significant increase in the respective lipoprotein and total lipid levels. For example, genetic polymorphism of apo E results in three main isoforms: E-2, E-3 and E-4. The affinity for apo E-2 with apo E receptors is low and consequently apo E-2 homozygosity is associated with hyperlipidaemia.

Lipid metabolism

Introduction

Triglycerides and cholesterol may be either derived from dietary sources or synthesized by the body *de novo*. Metabolism of lipids may therefore be considered as involving either exogenous or endogenous transport of lipids to tissues. In addition, the process of 'reverse cholesterol transport' occurs which allows removal of excess cholesterol from tissues and involves high-density lipoprotein. The latter can be considered as performing a 'scavenging' function, collecting cholesterol from the tissues and transporting it back to the liver.

The exogenous pathway

This pathway involves absorption and metabolism of dietary fat within the lumen of the small intestine (Figure 1.4). Dietary triglyceride and cholesterol are emulsified by the action of bile salts within the lumen of the small intestine, producing small micelles with a hydrophobic core of fat. The action of pancreatic lipases on triglycerides produces monoglycerides and hence causes the release of free fatty acids. Within the cells of the intestinal mucosal layer, the fatty acid cells are reconverted to triglyceride which then passes into the circulation where the triglyceride and cholesterol esters are incorporated into the largest lipoprotein particle, the chylomicron. Non-polar free cholesterol, together with apolipoproteins, form the outside of the particle.

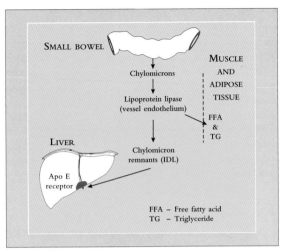

Figure 1.4 Exogenous lipid pathway.

Chylomicrons travel via the lymphatic system to the lymphatic duct. Circulating chylomicrons are degraded by the enzyme lipoprotein lipase, which is attached by heparan sulphate to the vascular endothelial lining and adipose tissue capillaries. The action of this enzyme releases glycerol and free fatty acids which are then taken up as an energy source by tissues or may be stored for fuel in fat. The removal of triglyceride from chylomicrons leaves a more dense remnant particle containing mainly cholesterol and cholesterol ester. This is removed by receptors in the liver that recognise apo E on the surface of the remnant particle. The enzyme also requires apo C-11 as a co-factor. During the metabolism of chylomicrons to chylomicron remnant particles, cholesterol, phospholipid and apolipoproteins A and C leave the particle to join the HDL pool.

Chylomicrons are not normally present in the fasting state, but if present in significant quantity, they may form a creamy layer on the top of a plasma sample due to their low density.

The endogenous pathway

Cholesterol and triglyceride may both be synthesized in the liver and transported to the tissues as endogenous lipid, packaged into VLDL (Figure 1.5). After acquisition of apo C from HDL, VLDL interacts with lipoprotein lipase to form the more cholesterol-rich intermediate-density lipoprotein (IDL). This lipoprotein is either removed by the apo E receptor or is converted to LDL. LDL, which is dense in cholesterol, may be removed from the circulation by LDL receptors in the liver or it may be taken up by peripheral tissues. This peripheral uptake of LDL is fundamental to the process of atherogenesis and has led to LDL being termed the 'atherogenic' lipoprotein.

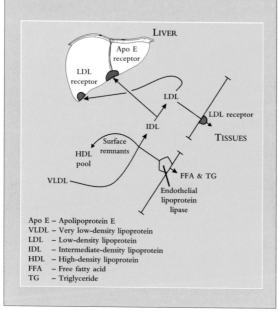

Figure 1.5 **Endogenous lipid pathway.**

Lipoprotein (Lp) (a) is similar in structure to LDL but also contains apo B. Lp(a) shows structural homology with fibrinogen and may link with the processes of atherosclerosis and thrombosis. Elevated levels of Lp(a) are associated with increased cardiovascular risk, particularly if LDL is also raised.

This complex pathway involving HDL is the mechanism by which circulating cholesterol can be excreted. HDL transports cholesterol from peripheral tissues, and lipoproteins back to the liver (Figure 1.6). Newly formed HDL is synthesized in the liver, or intestinal cells, and may receive cholesterol in the circulation to form mature HDL. The mature HDL particle transfers cholesterol back to chylomicron remnants or IDL which may be cleared directly by hepatic receptors. HDL's reverse cholesterol transport has led to it being called the 'protective' lipoprotein.

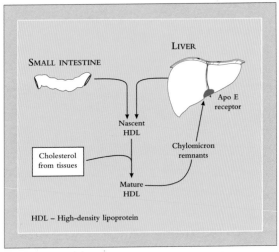

Figure 1.6 **Reverse cholesterol transport.**

The LDL receptor

The LDL receptor binds LDL and VLDL remnants, such as IDL, and synthesis occurs in response to a fall in cellular free cholesterol concentration (Figure 1.7). Following binding to the receptor, LDL particles are internalised and then undergo lysosomal hydrolysis. The resulting increase in intracellular cholesterol results in a number of changes. The synthesis of 3-hydroxy 3-methylglutaryl-Co enzyme A (HMG-CoA) reductase is suppressed with resultant inhibition of intracellular cholesterol synthesis, whereas the activity of the cholesterol-esterifying enzyme ACAT (acyl-coenzyme A-cholesterol acyltransferase) is augmented allowing excess free cholesterol to be stored as cholesterol esters. LDL receptor synthesis is inhibited, reducing cellular influx of cholesterol. The majority of LDL clearance from the plasma is carried out by the liver, with 70% of clearance by LDL receptors. It is important to note that 30% of clearance is through non-receptor mediated pathways.

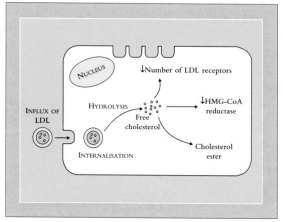

Figure 1.7 Cholesterol and the LDL receptor.

The enterohepatic circulation

Cholesterol provides the substrate for synthesis of bile salts in the liver. Of the cholesterol in bile, 50% is excreted and 50% of this is re-absorbed in the small intestine, whereas 95% of bile salts are re-absorbed and undergo enterohepatic re-circulation to the liver. The enterohepatic circulation provides a route for cholesterol excretion as well as a pathway for interruption to increase excretion of cholesterol, both directly or by increased conversion to bile acid in the hepatocyte.

MAJOR LIPID RISK FACTORS IN CORONARY HEART DISEASE

Atheroma formation

The onset of atherosclerosis occurs early in life with diffuse, regular thickening of the arteriole intima in childhood. The smooth appearance of the arteriolar tree may be altered during teenage years with formation of nodular aggregates or cushions of fibroelastic tissue which are termed 'fatty streaks'. Fatty streaks are collections of lipid, mainly cholesterol esters, in macrophages and smooth muscle cells (foam cells), deposited in the intima of an artery. They are present by the time of adolescence and are found in the cerebral and coronary arteries, and the aorta. Although it is assumed that fatty streaks are the precursors of established atherosclerosis, the location of fatty streaks within the main arteries shows little correlation with that of the fibrous plaques.

Fibrous plaques are white lesions that usually protrude into the vessel lumen (Figure 2.1). They consist of a core of cholesterol, cholesterol ester, phospholipid and necrotic

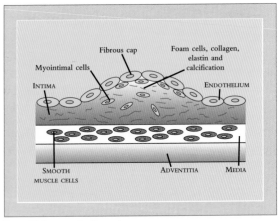

Figure 2.1 Structure of a fibrous plaque.

cells, covered by a fibrous cap of elastin and collagen. In elderly people these may calcify.

A key event in the formation of the fibrous plaque is smooth muscle cell proliferation from the media of the arteriole. Proliferation of modified smooth muscle cells is a process that is central to the main theories of atheroma formation. Another characteristic process is the formation of foam cells which contain a large quantity of lipid. These arise from the necrosis of smooth muscle cells which take up lipid. The clinical sequelae of atherosclerosis occur when complications of the fibrous plaque give rise to slow, or sudden, vascular occlusion. Mechanisms by which these two events may occur are listed in Figure 2.2. The most common sites of atherosclerosis and fibrous plaque formation giving rise to clinical sequelae are the coronary, cerebral (included carotid), aortic, femoral and peripheral circulation of the legs.

- **Rupture**

- **Mural thrombus on the plaque surface**

- **Haemorrhage into the plaque**

- **Calcification**

Figure 2.2 Complications of the atherosclerotic plaque leading to vascular occlusion.

The sclerotic lesion contains both LDL and apo B of LDL at concentrations directly proportional to those in the serum. The process by which monocytes take up lipid and become foam cells may involve the uptake of modified LDL-cholesterol via specific receptors which do not recognise native LDL-cholesterol. The modification appears to involve peroxidation of polyunsaturated fatty acids in LDL lipids, a process which may be inhibited by circulating plasma antioxidants. Oxidised LDL attracts circulating monocytes, inhibits the motility of tissue macrophages and is directly cytotoxic to endothelial cells (Figure 2.3).

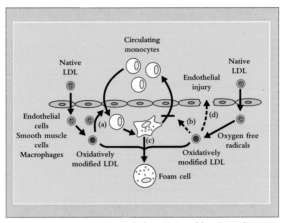

Figure 2.3 The mechanisms by which the oxidation of low-density lipoprotein (LDL) may contribute to atherogenesis are: (a) the recruitment of circulating monocytes by means of the chemotactic factor present in oxidised LDL, but absent in native LDL; (b) inhibition by oxidised LDL of the motility of resident macrophages and therefore their ability to leave the intima; (c) enhanced rate of uptake of oxidised LDL by resident macrophages, leading to the generation of foam cells; (d) cytotoxicity of oxidised LDL, leading to loss of endothelial integrity. Adapted with permission.

The theories of atheroma resulting in the endothelial cell injury hypothesis are still current. Endothelial cell injury causes a sequence of events involving cellular dysfunction and separation. This ultimately leads to exposure of the sub-endothelial connective tissue. Platelets and macrophages attach to this region and release growth factors, including platelet and macrophage-derived growth factors which may then cause smooth muscle proliferation.

Lipid accumulation is an important component of atherosclerosis.

In populations in the Western World atherosclerosis manifests commonly as coronary heart disease as the major cause of death, but also leads to substantial morbidity from angina and cardiac failure. In addition, there is considerable morbidity and mortality from cerebrovascular and peripheral vascular disease. Table 2.1 demonstrates the devastating effect of CHD in various western populations. It accounts for 37–50% of all mortality and approximately

Country	CVD deaths per 100,000 population	Total CVD deaths as percentage of all causes
UK	578	49
France	367	37
Italy	428	46
Spain	345	45
Canada	310	43
USA	414	48
Japan	247	39

CVD – Cardiovascular disease

Table 2.1 **Deaths due to cardiovascular disease in different countries.**

25% of all cause mortality under the age of 65 years. In the USA, 500,000 people per year suffer myocardial infarction with a 30% mortality, and 300,000 individuals undergo coronary artery bypass grafting surgery. In the United Kingdom in 1992, CHD accounted for 26% of all deaths in England and 12% of deaths that were related to stroke.

There is evidence, however, that mortality from coronary heart disease is reducing in patients under the age of 75 in some countries. For example, in the USA, CHD mortality rates have almost halved during the period 1968 to 1988 in subjects under the age of 75. In contrast, the CHD death rate in the United Kingdom has only shown a minor decline since the late 1970s (Figure 2.4). There are also marked ethnic differences. The Asian population in England, for example, has a particularly high CHD risk and a high prevalence of insulin resistance, while Afro-Caribbeans are particularly prone to stroke, rather than CHD.

Estimates of the cost of hospital care and losses of production due to sickness and death as a result of

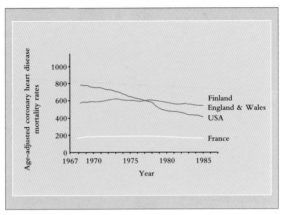

Figure 2.4 **Male coronary heart disease mortality rates 1967–1985.**

cardiovascular disease have been assessed by the United
Kingdom Office of Health Economics. These are estimated
to equal 1.6% of gross domestic product, 2.5% of total NHS
expenditure, a total cost estimated at £481 million (in 1987),
and 35 million lost working days in 1991. Similar figures for
cardiovascular health care are found in the USA, where the
total costs have been estimated at $100 billion.

Risk factors for coronary heart disease

The largest population studies relating to serum
cholesterol and lipoprotein concentrations in apparently
healthy populations have been performed in the USA.
These studies show a clear relationship between total
cholesterol and CHD mortality (Figure 2.5).

Risk factors for CHD are generally divided into those
which can be modified and those which cannot. This is
obviously important from the point of view of strategies for
prevention of CHD (Figure 2.6). Although total cholesterol
and LDL-cholesterol are powerful risk factors for CHD, the
other non-lipid related risk factors have long been
established as independent risk factors, some of which may
be modifiable. Prevention strategies need to consider all
risks and, in particular, the fact that when more than one
risk factor occurs in the same individual, the effect of

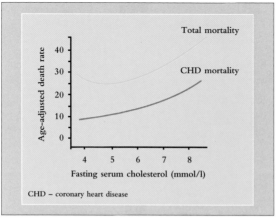

Figure 2.5 Mortality and cholesterol levels (data adapted from the MRFIT study).

Non-modifiable	Modifiable
Genetics	Hypertension
Age	Diabetes
Male sex	Smoking
Family history	Physical activity
	Obesity
	Low HDL-cholesterol
	Elevated triglycerides
	Elevated LDL-cholesterol

Figure 2.6 Known risk factors for coronary heart disease.

individual risks upon overall cardiovascular risk is multiplicative rather than additive.

Cholesterol and coronary heart disease

There is a strong positive relationship between cholesterol and CHD which is maintained across populations with differing cholesterol concentrations, as shown in the Seven Countries Study. The Multiple Risk

Factor Intervention Trial (MRFIT) (Figure 2.5) showed a powerful relationship between cholesterol and CHD with a flat curve up to a cholesterol of 5.2 mmol/l, but with a gradual increase in CHD mortality rate to 6.5 mmol/l. Above 6.5 mmol/l serum cholesterol, the mortality rate shows a steep increase. The association of LDL-cholesterol, however, is even stronger than that for cholesterol. As demonstrated in the Framingham Heart Study (Figure 2.7), the relationship between total or LDL-cholesterol level and CHD risk is continuous, with no strict cut-off point between levels that are safe and those that are high risk.

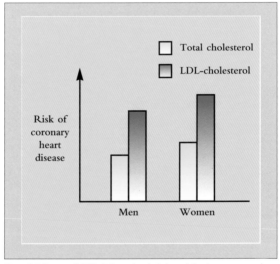

Figure 2.7 Impact of LDL-cholesterol and cholesterol levels on coronary heart disease risk in men and women in the Framingham Study.

Triglyceride and HDL in coronary heart disease

The association of fasting serum triglyceride and CHD remains controversial, although triglyceride does not appear to be an independent risk factor. Triglyceride may, however, play a more prominent role in special patient groups such as diabetic subjects.

There is also evidence from the Framingham Heart Study that the combination of an elevated serum triglyceride with a reduced HDL-cholesterol is strongly associated with CHD for both men and women (Figure 2.8). HDL promotes the transport of extra-hepatic cholesterol back to the liver for excretion. This reversed cholesterol transport may therefore explain the strong association of low HDL with CHD, with a higher HDL being cardioprotective. Reduced HDL-cholesterol as an independent risk factor for CHD has been demonstrated in several studies.

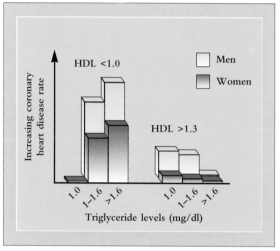

Figure 2.8 The relationship of coronary heart disease, low HDL and triglyceride values derived from the Framingham study.

Non-lipid risk factors and coronary heart disease

These risk factors include hypertension, diabetes mellitus, smoking and obesity, and are modifiable (Figure 2.6), in contrast to factors such as age, sex and family history. Several of these modifiable risk factors appear to occur as a cluster in the same patient and this combination has been termed the 'Metabolic Syndrome' or 'Syndrome X' (Figure 2.9).

Reaven hypothesized that this co-occurrence of risk factors might relate to an underlying primary problem – insulin resistance. There is now good evidence that insulin

- Insulin resistance

- Hyperinsulinaemia

- Increased serum triglycerides

- Decreased HDL-cholesterol

- Hypertension

- Obesity

Figure 2.9 **Major components of 'Syndrome X' – the chronic cardiovascular risk syndrome.**

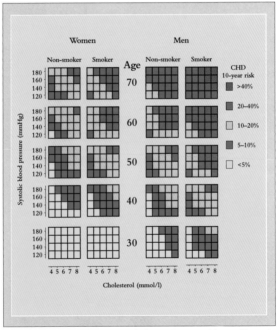

Figure 2.10 **An example of charts for calculation of coronary risk, according to the presence of multiple risk factors (adapted from the Combined Task Force of the European Societies chart).**

resistance is indeed the primary abnormality in the majority of Type 2 diabetic patients, but the relationship is more controversial with regard to hypertension.

Evidence from various studies has allowed risk factor profiles to be drawn up estimating the 10-year risk of developing ischaemic heart disease. An example of this is from the Combined Task Force coronary risk chart (Figure 2.10). It is important to stress that the presence of multiple risk factors multiplies coronary heart and cerebrovascular disease risk.

2

HYPERLIPIDAEMIA

This condition is present when plasma lipid levels are abnormal. The following terminology is used:

Type	LDL-cholesterol	Triglycerides	Terminology
A	↑	Normal	Hypercholesterolaemia
B	Normal	↑	Hypertriglyceridaemia
C	↑	↑	Combined hyperlipidaemia
D	↑↑	↑↑↑	Marked combined hyperlipidaemia

(Low HDL levels also contribute a lipid abnormality)

The hyperlipidaemias may be genetic, primary or secondary to other disorders.

What lipid levels are normal?

Studies of serum cholesterol in western populations show a mean value of 5.5–6 mmol/l. The increased risk of CHD shows a continuous relationship with increasing serum cholesterol such that cardiovascular risk starts to rise at cholesterol above 5.2 mmol/l (Figure 2.5). Thus the normal statistical methods of calculating a normal range for lipid values are meaningless. The statistical and epidemiological approach taken together have led to the concept of two threshold levels for serum cholesterol, with an ideal value being <5.2 mmol/l while levels above 6.5 mmol/l are clearly elevated. The clinical significance of values between 5.2 and 6.5 mmol/l is dependent on other factors, particularly the presence or absence of CHD, and of other concomitant cardiovascular risk factors.

In the case of serum triglycerides, disease risk is less clearly defined and thus the definition of normality is more difficult. The European Atherosclerosis Society (EAS) guidelines suggest that fasting levels of triglyceride >2.3 mmol/l are abnormal, although some authorities regard 2.1 mmol/l as an upper limit. An HDL-cholesterol level of <1 mmol/l, although varying according to analytical technique, is also considered abnormal. Table 3.1 contains the cut-off points suggested by the EAS for cholesterol, HDL-cholesterol and triglyceride levels.

Hypercholesterolaemia	Cholesterol value (mmol/l)	
Mild	>5.2 to ≤6.5	
Moderate	>6.5 to ≤7.8	
Severe	>7.8	
Hypertriglyceridaemia	Triglyceride value (mmol/l)	
Moderate	>2.3 to <4.6	
Severe	>4.6	
HDL-cholesterol	Concentration (mmol/l)	
	Men	Women
Reduced risk	>1.5	>1.7
Increased risk	<1.0	<1.2
High risk	<0.8	<1.0

Table 3.1 European Atherosclerosis Society lipid values (1992).

Clinical classification of hyperlipidaemias

Hyperlipidaemias are commonly classified by defined phenotypes which are useful as a guide to therapy. The Fredricksson classification of hyperlipidaemia is based upon the pattern of lipoprotein abnormality (Table 3.2). This categorisation takes no account of whether hyperlipidaemias are primary or secondary.

Type	Chylomicrons	VLDL	IDL	LDL	Comment
I	++++	N	N	Low	Very rare
IIa	-	N	N	++	Familial hypercholesterolaemia
IIb	-	++	N,+	++	Combined hyperlipidaemia (cholesterol raised more than triglyceride)
III	+	+	+++	Low	Apo E defect (Marked elevation in triglyceride and less so in cholesterol)
IV	-	++	N	N	Isolated hypertriglyceridaemia
V	++++	+++	N	Low	Severe hypertriglyceridaemia and marked hypercholesterolaemia

N=normal; +=increased; -=absent

Table 3.2 The Fredricksson classification of hyperlipidaemia.

Primary hyperlipidaemias

Primary hyperlipidaemias are determined genetically and the site of the defect has been identified in a number of disorders. Frequently occurring hyperlipidaemias result from a combination of genetic and environmental factors. Table 3.3 summarises the primary hyperlipidaemias, some of which are rare.

The most common inherited or familial hyper-lipidaemia is familial hypercholesterolaemia. This condition is characterised by a raised plasma total and LDL-cholesterol due to impaired LDL receptor activity. The homozygous condition is characterised by an absence of LDL receptor

Disorder	Inheritance	Lipoprotein abnormality	Lipid elevation	Atherosclerosis risk
Familial hypercholesterolaemia	Autosomal dominant	LDL	C	Homozygous ++++ Heterozygous ++
Common polygenic hypercholesterolaemia	Polygenic	LDL	C	+
Hyperalphalipo-proteinaemia	Polygenic	HDL	C	-
Familial combined hyperlipidaemia	Polygenic	LDL, VLDL	C TG	++
Apo E-2 homozygosity (Type III hyperlipidaemia)	Polygenic	IDL	C TG	++
Familial hypertriglyceridaemia	Autosomal dominant	VLDL	TG	+
Apo C-II deficiency	Autosomal recessive	Chylomicrons	TG	-
Lipoprotein lipase deficiency	Autosomal recessive and sporadic	Chylomicrons	TG	-

C – Cholesterol
TG – Triglyceride

Table 3.3 **Primary hyperlipidaemias.**

activity, whereas in the more common heterozygous condition there are approximately 50% of the normal number of LDL receptors. Other common familial hypercholesterolaemias include apo E-2 homozygosity, occurring at a frequency of 1:100. The lipoprotein abnormality in this disorder is of the Fredricksson type 3 pattern, with an increase in circulating IDL. Familial combined hypertriglyceridaemia and polygenic hypercholesterolaemia are also common. Rare disorders include lipoprotein lipase deficiency, apo C-II deficiency and hyperalphalipoproteinaemia. These are, however, important to identify because of their implications for clinical management.

These are common and account for about 40% of the total prevalence of lipid abnormalities. The abnormalities are often reversible with appropriate management of the underlying condition, but if this is not the case then primary hyperlipidaemia should be considered. The most common causes of secondary hyperlipidaemia include:

- obesity \
- diabetes mellitus } often in association with Syndrome X
- excessive alcohol consumption
- thyroid, renal and liver disease
- iatrogenic e.g. thiazide diuretics
    beta-blockers
    steroids
    oral contraceptives

Clinical features of hyperlipidaemias

In a minority of patients with hyperlipidaemia, physical signs can suggest abnormalities, but the majority of patients are asymptomatic until they present with clinically evident atherosclerosis such as ischaemic heart disease, peripheral vascular, or cerebrovascular disease.

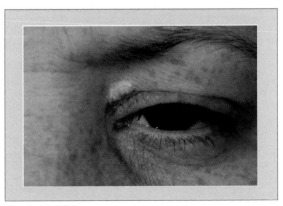

Figure 3.1 **Xanthelasma.**

The most common clinical signs associated with both primary and secondary causes of hyperlipidaemia are xanthelasma (Figure 3.1) and corneal arcus (Figure 3.2). Xanthelasma consist of products of LDL-cholesterol deposited in the palpable fissures. This abnormality is usually found in association with hypercholesterolaemia, but may be seen in the presence of normal lipid and lipoprotein levels. The causes of xanthelasma also include hypothyroidism, chronic liver disease and nephrotic syndrome.

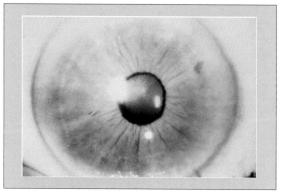

Figure 3.2 **Corneal arcus.**

Corneal arcus is a common physical sign best correlated with increasing age, so that the accuracy of this abnormality as a predictor of underlying hyperlipidaemia is poor. It is, however, seen in hyperlipidaemia associated with premature atherosclerosis and, if marked in people under the age of 60 years, lipid levels should be checked. Both corneal arcus and xanthelasma are non-specific clinical features of hyperlipidaemia. The non-specific and specific signs are listed in Figure 3.3.

The physical signs associated with primary hyperlipidaemia resulting from deficiencies of enzymes or receptors and apolipoprotein defects may include tendon xanthomata (Figure 3.4). These are pathological depositions of lipid in skin and tendons. The typical tendon xanthomata become more prominent with age, usually involving extensor tendons of the hands and achilles tendons. Less commonly the patella tendons and olecranon may be involved. These abnormalities strongly suggest familial hypercholesterolaemia.

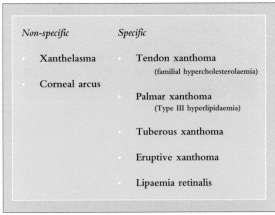

Non-specific	Specific
• Xanthelasma	• Tendon xanthoma (familial hypercholesterolaemia)
• Corneal arcus	• Palmar xanthoma (Type III hyperlipidaemia)
	• Tuberous xanthoma
	• Eruptive xanthoma
	• Lipaemia retinalis

Figure 3.3 Clinical features of the hyperlipidaemias.

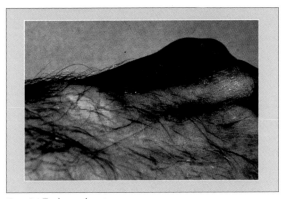

Figure 3.4 Tendon xanthomata.

Other physical signs found in patients with the rare homozygous familial hypercholesterolaemia and the more common Type III hyperlipidaemia (apo E-2 abnormalities) are planar or tuberous xanthomata. Tuberous or eruptive xanthomas (Figure 3.5) occur on the pressure areas, particularly the knees and elbows. As these lesions coalesce and enlarge they form into tuberous xanthomata. Patients

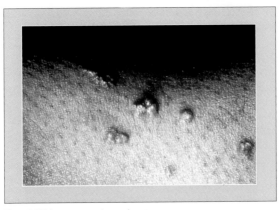

Figure 3.5 **Tuberous or eruptive xanthomata.**

with severe hypertriglyceridaemia (serum fasting triglycerides above 20 mmol/l) may show lipaemia retinalis where the retinovasculature have a creamy appearance (Figure 3.6). Hepatosplenomegaly, tenderness of the liver and spleen and abdominal pain may also be present. Pancreatitis may occur as a complication. Eruptive xanthomata are the characteristic skin lesions of severe hypertriglyceridaemia and appear as small, yellow papules typically on the arms, buttocks, and thighs (Figure 3.5).

3

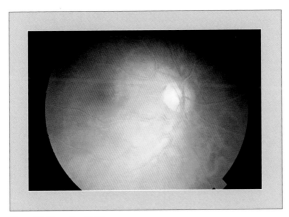

Figure 3.6 **Lipaemia retinalis.**

Despite the above, the major feature associated with hypercholesterolaemia and severe hypertriglyceridaemia is atherosclerosis, leading to a major vascular event. Though large vessel disease predominates, microvascular disease affecting the retinal circulation has a well established association with hypertriglyceridaemia and hypercholesterolaemia. This disease includes retinal vein occlusion, retinal artery occlusion and ischaemic optic neuropathy. Examples of these are shown in Figure 3.7 and 3.8.

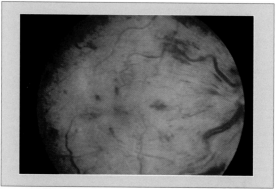

Figure 3.7 **Retinal vein occlusion.**

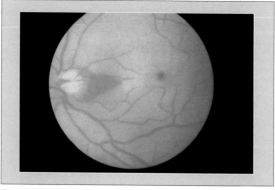

Figure 3.8 **Central retinal artery occlusion.**

Why treat lipid disorders?

As outlined previously, a number of clinical features may point to the diagnosis of hyperlipidaemia. As the common major sequelae of hypercholesterolaemia are atherosclerosis and clinical end-points, the major aim of treatment is to reduce the risk of atherosclerotic vascular disease. In addition, treatment of severe hypertriglyceridaemia reduces the risk of pancreatitis, and treatment of hyperlipidaemia reduces the risk of recurrence of retinovascular disease.

Does treating lipid disorders reduce atherosclerosis?

The evidence that cholesterol is a risk factor for CHD and atherosclerotic vascular disease comes from many studies and is well established. These include cohort studies of international comparisons between populations and intervention studies. The largest cohort study, the MRFIT study, clearly delineated the relationship between increasing serum cholesterol and CHD mortality (see Figure 2.5). Other studies have now confirmed this strong relationship. These studies have included the British Regional Heart Survey, which demonstrated that men with cholesterol in the highest quintile distribution (>7.2 mmol/l) had a 3.5 times greater risk of CHD compared with those in the lowest quintile (<5.5 mmol/l). The study also demonstrated an inverse association of CHD with increasing HDL-cholesterol. CHD risk was half as common in the highest quintile (>1.33 mmol/l) compared with the lowest quintile (<0.93 mmol/l). Multivariant analysis confirmed that both cholesterol and LDL-cholesterol are the predominant independent risk factors.

4

International comparison studies have strongly supported the role of increasing serum cholesterol and death rate from CHD amongst different populations (Figure 4.1). Studies of CHD risk in populations that migrate from an area of low incidence of CHD to one of high incidence have demonstrated up to a 3-fold increase in CHD rate. This was emphasised in a study of Japanese people migrating to either Hawaii or San Francisco.

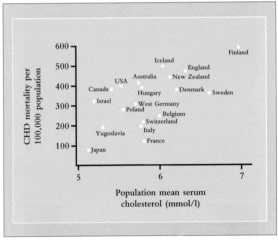

Figure 4.1 Ischaemic heart disease mortality and serum cholesterol levels in different populations.

Controversy still persists regarding the atherogenicity of triglyceride-rich lipoproteins and the importance of hypertriglyceridaemia in CHD. This may reflect the number of different mechanisms by which the triglyceride-rich lipoproteins may be atherogenic, procoagulant and antifibrinolytic. Epidemiological studies have assessed the associations between serum triglycerides and the risk of development of CHD in a prospective manner. However, these studies have not confirmed triglycerides and triglyceride-rich lipoproteins as independent risk factors, particularly when HDL, serum cholesterol and total cholesterol levels are included.

The early intervention studies assessing the treatment and reduction of lipid levels with drug or dietary therapy gave rise to controversy and concern at their failure to show a reduction in all-cause mortality. In addition, some of the drug intervention trials showed apparent increases in death from other causes, with a suggestion of an increase in violent and accidental deaths in several studies. Failure to demonstrate a reduction in total mortality from all causes was due, in part, to a lack of power in study design, and also because the reduction of cholesterol was only about 10%. This may be explained by the relative lack of efficacy of dietary regimens, resins and fibrates in cholesterol-lowering when compared to the powerful 'statin' agents. Newer intervention trials using statins (HMG-CoA reductase inhibitors) have achieved much greater reductions in cholesterol (20–30%), thereby improving the potential for greater reductions in cardiovascular events and mortality from all causes.

The evidence of benefit from lipid-lowering therapy derives from two catagories of trials. Firstly, the major angiographic trials of lipid-lowering in patients with coronary heart disease, and secondly, prospective studies of lipid-lowering drug therapy on the incidence of fatal and non-fatal myocardial infarction in primary or secondary prevention. In this latter category, the introduction of the statins has considerably strengthened the evidence for the major benefit of lipid-lowering on coronary artery disease mortality and morbidity and the reduction of all-cause mortality.

Thirteen major angiographic trials of lipid-lowering therapy in patients with coronary heart disease have been performed. These involved randomised comparisons between diet alone or diet combined with various lipid-lowering drug therapies. The early trials used cholestyramine and nicotinic acid. The largest trial used partial ileal bypass (Program on the Surgical Control of Hyperlipidaemias (POSCH)), whilst others have used exercise, and more recent ones have used statins. A summary of the frequency of coronary lesion progression

4

Group	Regression (% of patients)	Progression
Treatment	18	29
Control	9	44

	Cholesterol (lowering %)	LDL
Mean effect of lipid-lowering (treatment versus control groups)	-21%	-31%

Table 4.1 Summary of progression or regression of coronary artery lesions in the angiographic studies with lipid-lowering.

and regression in these trials is shown in Table 4.1. There was a significant reduction in cardiovascular events and in the need for revascularisation in the majority of the studies – there were changes in the progression of coronary, as well as carotid artery disease. These changes were associated with an approximate 30% reduction in mean LDL-cholesterol levels, whereas the reduction in triglyceride was relatively small at 2.5%.

There have now been 11 large prospective lipid-lowering trials which have included clinical end-points. These have included six primary and five secondary prevention trials to date. These are summarised in Table 4.2. Despite concerns that there was no reduction in overall total morbidity in the early trials of both primary and secondary prevention, there was a significant reduction in non-fatal myocardial infarction. Three of these trials considerably strengthened the evidence that lipid-lowering drug therapy is of benefit. These were 4S (Scandinavian Simvastatin Survival Study), WOSCOPS (the West of Scotland Coronary Prevention Study) and the CARE (Cholesterol and Recurrent Events) study. The 4S and CARE studies have demonstrated the impressive treatment effects of cholesterol-lowering in reducing subsequent

Study	Duration of trial (years)	Treatment	CHD incidence % reduction
Primary Prevention			
LA Veterans Study	8	Diet alone	23
WHO Co-operative Trial	5	Clofibrate	20
LRC-CCP Trial	7.4	Cholestyramine	19
Helsinki Heart Study	5	Gemfibrozil	34
WOSCOPS	4.9	Pravastatin	32
AFCAPS	5.2	Lovastatin	37
Secondary Prevention			
Coronary Drug Project	5	Niacin	26
Stockholm Study	5	Clofibrate and nicotinic acid	26
4S	4.9–6.3	Simvastatin	34
CARE Study	3.4–6.2	Pravastatin	24
LIPID Study	6	Pravastatin	23

Table 4.2 Prevention trials of lipid-lowering therapies.

cardiovascular events in patients with existing coronary heart disease, i.e. *as secondary prevention.* In the 4S trial, 4,444 men and women aged 35 to 70 with a previous history of angina pectoris or myocardial infarction, and a serum cholesterol of 5.5–8 mmol/l were randomised after a period of diet therapy to receive simvastatin 20–40 mg daily or placebo. Simvastatin lowered LDL-cholesterol by 25% and triglycerides by 10% with an elevation of HDL-cholesterol of 8%. There was a 42% decrease in coronary heart disease mortality over a mean treatment period of 5.4 years.

4

Importantly, there were no differences in non-cardiovascular causes of death versus placebo and there was a significant reduction in overall mortality in the intervention group.

The other secondary prevention trial, CARE, was a double-blind investigation of pravastatin in patients with previous myocardial infarction. In contrast to the 4S study, the entry total cholesterol of all subjects was ≤6.2 mmol/l, and LDL-cholesterol ranged from 3 to 4.5 mmol/l with triglyceride <4 mmol/l. The mean total cholesterol at entry in the study was only 5.4 mmol/l. This trial agreed with the 4S results and showed that a 20% reduction in LDL-cholesterol, achieved on a statin, resulted in a 24% reduction in coronary heart disease death or non-fatal recurrent myocardial infarction. Importantly, this study clarified a target level of blood cholesterol. When baseline cholesterol was 5 mmol/l or less, there was no evidence of clinical benefit from its reduction. In addition, cost-effectiveness strategies in both these trials resulted in a significant reduction in coronary revascularisation procedures, including coronary artery bypass grafting surgery and angioplasty.

The most recent and largest trial to report was the LIPID study (Long-term Intervention with Pravastatin in Ischaemic Heart Disease). This study again demonstrated an impressive 24% reduction in death from coronary heart disease after 6 years treatment with pravastatin, compared with placebo, in 9000 men and women (aged 31–75 years) with a history of heart attack or hospitalisation for unstable angina. Significant lowering of total mortality, need for cardiac surgery, and stroke were observed, with risk reductions of between 20% and 29% in the pravastatin-treated group.

These three large secondary prevention studies confirm beyond question the value of lipid-lowering in the context of secondary prevention of coronary heart disease.

The recently published study, WOSCOPS, has confirmed the potential benefit of statin treatment in primary prevention. This trial was of 6,595 men, aged between 45 and 64 years of age, with an average baseline cholesterol of 7 mmol/l and no history of previous coronary heart disease. They were randomised to a 5-year treatment period of pravastatin or placebo. The trial demonstrated a 26% mean fall in plasma LDL-cholesterol and a decreased risk of fatal or non-fatal myocardial infarction by 31% and of all-cause mortality by 22%. The Air Force Texas Coronary Atherosclerosis Prevention Study (AFCAPS/TexCAPS) has re-emphasised the WOSCOPS trial results in 6,605 subjects with mean total cholesterol of 5.7 mmol/l, and comprising a low risk group, treated for 5 years with lovastatin. This trial demonstrated a 25% mean reduction in LDL-cholesterol, with a 37% reduction of primary cardiovascular end-points.

These landmark studies provide a firm new evidence base on which to make clinical decisions with regard to the use of lipid-lowering drug therapy for either *primary* or *secondary* prevention. Estimates of the number of patients treated with statins over a 5-year period to prevent a cardiovascular event can be calculated from the trials. These

Drug	Condition	Estimated no. of patients
Aspirin	Transient ischaemic attack	6
Aspirin	Post MI	12
ACE-inhibitors	Congestive heart failure	8
Warfarin	Atrial fibrillation	7
Statins	*Secondary prevention* Post MI	10
	Angina	16
Statins	*Primary prevention* Asymptomatic + other risk factors	26
	Asymptomatic, ↑LDL only	42

4

Table 4.3 Estimates from the large intervention trials of the number of patients treated for 5 years to prevent a cardiovascular event.

calculations (Table 4.3) confirm that lipid-lowering using statin therapy is as efficacious as other established treatments, for example aspirin, ACE inhibitors and warfarin. Whilst these recent landmark studies have pointed the way forward, paradoxically they have also made further studies more difficult to perform owing to the ethical issues of a placebo arm in either primary or secondary prevention trials. The real challenge, however, is not in deciding which lipid lowering drug to use, or which patients to treat, but to determine whether treatment is cost-effective and at what threshold of risk should treatment be initiated.

STRATEGY FOR LIPID-SCREENING AND MANAGEMENT OF HYPERLIPIDAEMIA

Introduction

Most morbidity and mortality from coronary heart disease occurs in those with average rather than very high levels of cholesterol. In order to significantly affect the incidence of coronary heart disease, therefore, a number of approaches could be employed. The first, broad approach could be to reduce the mean cholesterol level in the population as a whole. The second, 'targeted' approach is to identify those subjects who would benefit from a more aggressive approach to cholesterol-lowering because of their increased overall cardiovascular risk. For this, four categories of subjects would need to be identified:

- Those with established coronary heart disease.
- Those with multiple risk factors, without coronary heart disease.

(In both, the benefit of lipid-lowering is well established)

- Those with elevated serum cholesterol sufficient to put them at increased absolute risk of coronary heart disease.
- Those with familial hyperlipidaemia.

The fourth category comprises a small percentage of the total population, but these subjects are extremely important to identify as they are at a higher risk for coronary heart disease than predicted by population and cohort studies.

The third category is more problematic. Data supporting the benefit of lipid-lowering drug therapy comes from the WOSCOPS study. Controversy, however, surrounds the cost-effectiveness of lipid-lowering in this particular group of subjects.

These four categories are recognised by a number of national and international guidelines for the screening and treatment of elevated serum cholesterol. As the benefits of lipid-lowering in patients with established coronary heart disease are now proven, guidelines for the management of hypercholesterolaemia in this clinical context are unanimous. There is still controversy about the benefits for other groups (i.e. primary prevention), as debate has moved from whether lipid-lowering is effective, to a cost-effectiveness argument related to the absolute risk of coronary heart disease in a particular subject. Guidelines therefore differ slightly in the target values of serum cholesterol for each group and also in the recommended approaches to screening for those at high risk.

Screening strategies

Population screening

This approach has been advocated in the USA and directed by the guidelines of the National Cholesterol Education Programme (NCEP). These guidelines advocate the measurement of serum cholesterol approximately once every 5 years in all adults aged over 20. All subjects are encouraged to know their cholesterol value, and to modify their diet and lifestyle if this is in excess of the 'ideal' value of 5.2 mmol/l.

The population screening approach is the only reliable way to identify all those with genetic hyperlipidaemias, who may not have any clinical features of either hyperlipidaemia or cardiovascular disease. On the negative side, the resource implications of this approach are huge. Identification of a large group of people with moderately elevated cholesterol who may not be at greatly increased risk of cardiovascular disease is a potential problem, but is an inevitable consequence of such an approach. For these reasons, aggressive population screening is not universally accepted and, recently, a more limited approach has been advocated in the USA by the American College of Physicians.

In order to identify those in whom lipids should be measured without adopting a population screening method, a number of targeted approaches can be used. These include 'selective', 'family', and 'opportunistic' screening:

- Selective screening is used for those patients who have coronary heart disease, those who have two or more risk factors for coronary heart disease or those with clinical features of hyperlipidaemia.
- Family screening is used where a case of genetic hyperlipidaemia is identified, and other family members are screened for the disorder.
- The opportunistic approach is to perform screening, for example, at a well-person check, a routine employment medical examination, or to advise a cholesterol test for those consulting their general practitioner about an unrelated matter. Unless an informed decision is made on the basis of cardiovascular risk, this approach is just a limited form of population-based screening. If this method is adopted, it should not replace a detailed assessment of a subject's overall cardiovascular risk.

In the United Kingdom, the current trial evidence makes selective screening mandatory for those patients who have coronary heart disease. The potential of genetic hyperlipidaemia makes family screening a priority in clinical management. Opportunistic screening has been encouraged in the UK and has heightened awareness of the contribution of increased cholesterol levels to cardiovascular disease.

Who should be screened?

Whichever of the screening approaches is adopted, assessment of serum cholesterol in the following patient groups is mandatory:

- Those with established coronary heart disease.
- Those with multiple risk factors or a family history of

premature CHD (<55 years in male relatives or <65 years in female relatives).

- Those with clinical features or a family history of hyperlipidaemia.

Having identified those subjects who should have a lipid profile assessment, a random cholesterol measurement is initially all that is required. The difference in serum cholesterol in the post-prandial or fasting state is only about 3%. In contrast, triglycerides increase significantly post-prandially because of the release of chylomicrons into the circulation, and for definitive assessment these should be measured in the fasting sample.

How should lipids be measured?

Although cholesterol measurements can be made using 'near testing' equipment in a primary care setting, a laboratory estimation is required to confirm or refute the presence of hyperlipidaemia. If the initial serum cholesterol measurement is <5.2 mmol/l, further investigation is not required. If cholesterol is >5.2, a full fasting lipid profile, including measurement of cholesterol, triglyceride, and HDL-cholesterol, should be made on a fasting serum sample sent to the laboratory. This will identify whether there is an elevation of cholesterol alone, an elevation of other lipid components (for example triglyceride), or a reduction of HDL-cholesterol. HDL-cholesterol is an important measure, owing to its independent relationship with coronary heart disease risk. Elevated total cholesterol due to a greatly increased HDL may occur in the rare benign condition of hyperalphalipoproteinaemia. LDL-cholesterol levels may be calculated following measurement of the lipid profile according to the Friedewald formula, which is:

$$LDL\text{-}C = total\text{-}C - HDL\text{-}C - (triglyceride/2.2)$$

(all values in mmol/l)

Although calculation of LDL-cholesterol is not essential, the randomised prospective trials have calculated LDL-cholesterol reduction as the major measure, and hence LDL-cholesterol values are included in some national recommendations.

Assessment of risk

Assessment of absolute CHD risk requires the combination of all major CHD risk factors for an individual and their subsequent expression as an annual, 5- or 10-year risk. Study of epidemiological data, for example from the Procam Study and the Framingham Database, has allowed the calculation of absolute risk related to the presence of single or multiple risk factors for an individual. The level of absolute risk may then be calculated from a simple disc calculator or from more sophisticated computerised programmes which are currently becoming widely available. An example of the calculations is shown in Table 5.1, in which the different risks are shown for five 50-year-old male patients with hypercholesterolaemia. Included in this table is an estimate of the cost to prevent a myocardial infarction or coronary heart disease death for each individual.

Figure 2.10 (*Chapter 2*) shows an alternative way of expressing this data. This shows the risk factor profiles calculated by the Combined Task Force Coronary risk chart and estimates the 10-year risk of developing coronary heart disease. Despite the complexities of this calculation, the emphasis in all the major cardiovascular society lipid-lowering guidelines is to stress the importance of assessment of absolute coronary heart disease risk before initiating therapy. The problems with this type of approach are that the charts are complicated for clinical use, and that they take no account of the presence of genetic hyperlipidaemia which may confer increased cardiovascular risk above that reported in the chart.

All five examples of 50-year-old patients illustrated in Table 5.1 should be eligible for cholesterol-lowering drug treatment according to the guidelines of the British Hyperlipidaemia Association and the NCEP, provided their hypercholesterolaemia proves resistant to dietary therapy.

Patient E, who has evidence of coronary heart disease, is at a 40% risk of coronary heart disease death after 10 years. The cost, therefore, of prevention of myocardial infarction or death is lower than in patient A, who has hypercholesterolaemia alone and no other risk factors. Although this reinforces the importance of assessment of absolute coronary heart disease risk in an individual subject, assessment has become particularly important in terms of cost, both to local budgets (e.g. general practitioners) and national expenditure.

Known cardiovascular risk factors	Patients (male, 50 years of age)				
	A	B	C	D	E
Cholesterol (mmol/l)	8	8	8	8	8
HDL–cholesterol (mmol/l)	1.5	1.5	1.0	1.0	0.7
Hypertension	–	–	–	+	+
Angina	–	–	–	–	+
Diabetes mellitus	–	–	–	–	+
Smoking	–	–	+	+	+
Positive family history*	–	+	+	+	+
10-year absolute risk (%)	A	B	C	D	E
Myocardial infarction	5	7	31	53	100
Cardiovascular death	1	2	9	14	40
10-year reduction in absolute risk (%) with statin treatment					
Myocardial infarction	2	3	10	16	35
Cardiovascular death	<1	<1	3	5	18
Approximate cost (per £1000) of prevention of:					
Each myocardial infarction	250	190	44	24	11
Each cardiovascular death	1,100	800	200	100	24

*Family history of premature coronary heart disease.

Table 5.1 Example risk benefit analysis of five 50-year-old subjects with primary hypercholesterolaemia.

The Standing Medical Advisory Committee (SMAC) in the UK has recently emphasised priorities for lipid-lowering with drug therapy. They suggested, however, that for people without symptomatic coronary heart disease, drug prescription for lipid-lowering should only be used in those subjects who have a high cholesterol level and a risk of a major coronary event (myocardial infarction or death from CHD) of 3% per year or more. This is a 15% 5-year risk or a 30% 10-year risk. Thus, in the five 50-year-old patients shown in Table 5.1, patients C, D, and E would fulfil these criteria based on their absolute risk of myocardial infarction of 31% to 100%. In contrast, no lipid-lowering therapy would be advised in patients A and B. This is despite these subjects being similar to those studied in the WOSCOPS study with a lower absolute risk of myocardial infarction over 10 years of between 5% and 7%.

The publication by the SMAC also included tables showing serum cholesterol concentration conferring an estimated risk of coronary events according to the presence

(Primary prevention) Mean serum cholesterol (mmol/l)

Hypertension	+	+	+	No	+	No
Smoking	+	No	+	+	No	No
Diabetes	+	+	+	+	+	No
LVM on ECG	+	+	No	No	No	No
Age (years)						
70					5.5	6.0
					5.5	6.4
	5.5	5.5	5.5	5.5	5.7	6.8
					6.1	7.3
62					6.5	7.8
60				5.6	6.9	8.3
				6.1	7.4	8.9
58	5.5	5.5	5.5	6.5	8.0	
				5.9	7.0	8.6
52				6.3	7.6	9.3
50				6.9	8.2	
				7.5	8.9	
	5.5			8.2		
			5.8	9.0		
42			6.4			
40			7.1			
			7.9			
36	6.0		8.8			
	6.7					
32	7.0					
30	8.7					
<29						

(Serum cholesterol conferring estimated risk of coronary events of 3%/year)

Table 5.2a Serum cholesterol levels and estimated risk of coronary events (men).

(Primary prevention) Mean serum cholesterol (mmol/l)

Age (years)	Hypertension + / Smoking + / Diabetes + / LVM on ECG +	+ / No / + / +	+ / + / + / No	No / + / + / No	+ / No / + / No	No / No / + / No
Hypertension	+	+	+	No	+	No
Smoking	+	No	+	+	No	No
Diabetes	+	+	+	+	+	+
LVM on ECG	+	+	No	No	No	No
70						6.0
	5.5	5.5	5.5	5.5	5.5	6.4
					5.7	6.8
					6.1	7.3
62					6.5	7.8
60			5.5	5.6	6.9	8.2
	5.5	5.5		6.1	7.4	8.9
				6.5	8.0	
			5.9	7.0	8.6	
52			6.3	7.6	9.3	
50	5.5	5.5	6.9	8.2		
			7.5	8.9		
			8.2			
44		5.8	9.0			
42	5.8	6.4				
40	6.7	7.1				
38	8.0	7.9	(Serum cholesterol conferring estimated risk of coronary events of 3%/year)			
36	9.7	8.8				
<35						

Table 5.2b Serum cholesterol levels and estimated risk of coronary events (women).

of other known cardiovascular risk factors of ≥3% per year. The tables, one for men and one for women, are shown in Tables 5.2a and 5.2b. These tables have been criticised as there is no allowance for the presence of genetic hyperlipidaemia, particularly familial hypercholesterolaemia, which confers a major risk for coronary heart disease. In addition, no allowance for HDL-cholesterol values has been included, and diabetic subjects who have a three to four times increased risk of myocardial infarction, particularly in the presence of proteinuria, when compared to non-diabetics, have an inappropriately high threshold for serum cholesterol level before drug therapy is initiated. Ethnic differences are not included, and there is no inclusion of the increasing risk according to actual blood pressure levels of an individual.

The SMAC recommendations and the Sheffield table have emphasised the importance of calculation of *absolute* risk. More recently, computerised programmes are becoming available to calculate absolute risk for routine clinical practice. An example of the information required to perform this calculation and risk analysis performed in the laboratory is shown in Table 5.3 (from the Framingham equation and courtesy of Dr A Jones and Dr W Bartlett, Chemical Pathology, Birmingham Heartlands Hospital).

[A]

CHD risk request

Does NOT apply to patients with ischaemic heart disease, peripheral vascular disease or genetic hyperlipidaemia.

Age............(30–74 years only)   Sex: M   F
Systolic BP...............mmHg   *mean of last 2 readings*
Smoker   Yes   No   *No=not for at least 12 months*
Diabetes   Yes   No
LVH   Yes   No   Don't know

[B]

Coronary heart disease risk analysis

Age: 66 years	Cigarette smoker: No
Sex: Male	Patient diabetic: Yes
Systolic BP: 170 mmHg	ECG shows LVH: No

Results: Cholesterol = 5.3 mmol/l (3.6–6.5)
             HDL–cholesterol = 1.00 mmol/l (0.60–1.60)

             Ten-year coronary heart disease risk = 31.3%

Risk calculated using the Framingham equation.
Calculation valid for subjects aged 30 to 74 years only.
Does not apply to those with ischaemic heart disease or genetic hyperlipidaemia.

Table 5.3 **Assessment of cardiovascular risk calculated from the Framingham equation: information required from the clinician [A] and an example of coronary risk analysis [B].**

The recent Joint British Recommendations in the Prevention of Coronary Heart Disease have emphasised this latter computerised approach in clinical practice. In our unit, this is our standard practice. As with other methods of absolute cardiovascular risk assessment, approximation is required for non-white ethnic populations and to estimate the increased risk associated with proteinurea. The upper age range is 74 years of age.

In most cases, hyperlipidaemia is diagnosed by finding abnormal lipid levels and may be either primary or secondary to a number of conditions (*Chapter 3*). Appropriate investigations (Table 5.4) should exclude

Assessment	Action
Presence of clinical signs of hyperlipidaemia;	
Hypercholesterolaemia: arcus senillis, xanthelasma, xanthoma	Fasting cholesterol and triglyceride estimation
	Calculation of LDL-cholesterol
Hypertriglyceridaemia:	Assessment of HDL-cholesterol
Eruptive xanthoma, lipaemia retinalis	Lipoprotein electrophoresis (for typing)
	Other tests:
	Apolipoprotein E & C isoforms
	Lipoprotein lipase activity
Degree of obesity	Determine Body Mass Index
Presence of other risk factors	
Hypertension	Check blood pressure. Avoid thiazides
Diabetes mellitus	Check blood glucose, glycated haemoglobin, urine protein estimation
Smoking	History – discontinuation
Family history	History – random lipid levels check in other family members
Signs associated with secondary causes	
Liver disease	Liver function tests
Alcohol abuse	Liver function tests, amylase, gamma glutaryl transferase
Thyroid disease	Free T$_4$, TSH
Diabetes mellitus	Fasting blood glucose (glucose tolerance test)
Renal disease	Serum creatinine, urine protein estimation
Iatrogenic	e.g. thiazides, beta-blockers and prednisolone
Presence of clinical signs of large vessel disease	
Presence of bruits – carotid femoral	ECG
	? Ischaemic changes
Compromised left ventricle	? Ventricular hypertrophy
Signs of peripheral vascular disease	Doppler flow studies
	Carotid
	Peripheral
	Angiography

Table 5.4 Important points to consider in the clinical evaluation of a patient with newly diagnosed hyperlipidaemia.

underlying conditions as treatment may resolve the lipid abnormality.

In a small percentage of patients a number of clinical features of hyperlipidaemia may be recognised and should prompt investigation by measurement of fasting serum lipids. Some features are diagnostic of hyperlipidaemia while others (for example xanthelasma) are also seen in other conditions. Some features are virtually pathognomonic of specific genetic hyperlipidaemias while others indicate hyperlipidaemia, which may be due to a number of primary or secondary causes (Figures 3.5, 3.6 and Table 5.4). In the presence of abnormal physical signs of hyperlipidaemia (*Chapter 3*), it is imperative to take a family history and measure fasting lipids. Whilst these measures may confirm the 'familial' nature of the condition, assessment and appropriate management of other affected family members should confer significant long-term benefit.

Management of hyperlipidaemia

Based on the assessment of cardiovascular risk factors and cholesterol level, a classification of patients into one of three groups is possible:

- Those with established coronary heart disease.
- Those with multiple risk factors or with a genetic hyperlipidaemia.
- Those with isolated asymptomatic hyperlipidaemia.

These groups represent a gradient of absolute risk of a coronary event and therefore also absolute benefit to be achieved by cholesterol reduction as previously outlined. Treatment guidelines do differ in some details according to countries and expert panels, but there is broad agreement on the target levels for each of these groups of patients. The serum cholesterol value for therapy is now agreed at 4.8 mmol/l for *secondary* prevention. These target levels are shown in Table 5.5. However, with regard to *primary* prevention, the most recent guidelines have adopted the approach of calculating absolute coronary risk for an individual patient and basing treatment decisions on this

Risk	Target cholesterol level (mmol/l)
Modestly increased overall risk (especially if HDL-cholesterol >1.5 mmol/l)	5–6
Moderately increased overall risk	5

High overall risk
  - >1 non-lipid risk factor
  - Presence of existing coronary artery disease
  - Low HDL-cholesterol
	4.8–5

Table 5.5 Lipid targets according to overall risk (European Atherosclerosis Society).

result. An example of differing levels of risk in the population are shown in Table 5.6. The Standing Medical Advisory Committee advised intervention at >30% absolute risk, and whilst the recent joint British guidelines endorse this, the goal should now be based on a CHD risk of >15%, resulting in approximately 30% (under the age of 74 years) of the population eligible for treatment – a formidable number to treat and fund. This approach is demonstrated in Figure 5.1. Whilst the joint guidelines acknowledge the difficulties in achieving such treatment thresholds, a staged approach is advised to give top priority for prevention to patients with coronary heart disease or other major

	England (aged 30 to 74 years)		Scotland (aged 30 to 64 years)	
Absolute CHD risk (%)*	Men	Women	Men	Women
≥30	3	-	2	0.3
25 to 29	5	2	3	1
20 to 24	8	2	6	1
15 to 19	12	5	10	4

*Framingham function: absolute risk of non-fatal myocardial infarction and coronary death over 10 years.

Table 5.6 Percentage of men and women in England and Scotland at different levels of CHD risk (reproduced from Heart 1998; 80 (Suppl 2): S1–S29 with permission).

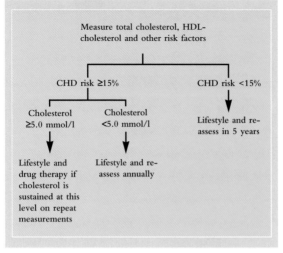

Figure 5.1 Absolute CHD risk and management of blood lipids in primary prevention of CHD and other atherosclerotic disease. CHD risk, non-fatal myocardial infarction and coronary deaths over 10 years (reproduced from Heart 1998; 80 (Suppl 2): S1–S29 with permission).

atherosclerotic disease. Subsequently, as resources allow, individuals with a 10-year absolute CHD risk of 15% or greater should be targeted. A similar approach is also suggested for the management of hypertension. Stringent treatment targets should be achieved for patients with a CHD risk of >15% over the next 10 years, as shown in Table 5.7. The recent summary of the recommendations of the Second Joint Task Force of European and other Societies on Coronary Prevention have largely endorsed the British guidelines, but have used an absolute CHD risk of 20% or greater as the threshold rather than 15% as in the joint British recommendations, shown in Figure 5.2.

With regard to hyperlipidaemia, a decision to treat with drugs will depend on absolute CHD risk, but this calculation may be less accurate and substantially underestimate the CHD risk. This particularly applies to individuals with familial hypercholesterolaemia in whom drug treatment is invariably necessary.

In subjects with newly diagnosed hyperlipidaemia, there are a number of important points to consider in their

BP less than:
> 140 mmHg Sytolic
> 85 mmHg Diastolic

Total cholesterol <5 mmol/l
(LDL-cholesterol <3 mmol/l)

Diabetes mellitus should be optimally controlled and BP
reduced to:
> <130 mmHg Systolic
> <80 mmHg Diastolic

Aspirin (75 mg) is recommended in individuals who are
older than 50 years and are either well-controlled
hypertensive patients or men at high risk of CHD

Table 5.7 Treatment targets in patients whose CHD risk is greater than 15% over
the next 10 years (adapted from Heart 1998; 80 (Suppl 2): S1–S29).

clinical assessment and investigation, and these are
summarised in Table 5.4. The more common secondary
causes of hyperlipidaemia must be excluded with
appropriate investigations, and only then may management
of hyperlipidaemia *per se* be undertaken.

Non-pharmacological management

All guidelines suggest initial management with non-
pharmacological treatment alone for approximately
3 months unless severe or rare genetic disorders are
identified.

Following initial assessment of a subject with newly
diagnosed hyperlipidaemia, the patient should be
encouraged to:

- stop smoking.
- reduce alcohol intake to safe levels.
- increase exercise.
- lose weight if appropriate.

All cases should be advised on dietary treatment. The
NCEP describes a Step 1 diet which is appropriate for the
population as a whole, together with lifestyle modifications
such as smoking cessation and regular exercise. The Step 1
diet, along with the more restrictive Step 2 diet, is shown in

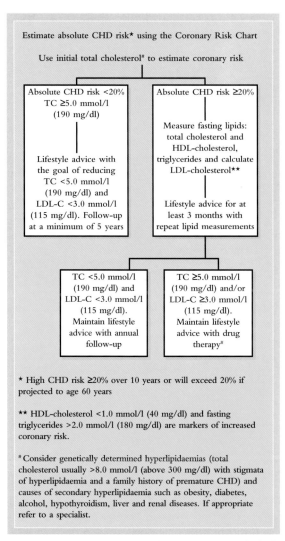

Estimate absolute CHD risk* using the Coronary Risk Chart

Use initial total cholesterol# to estimate coronary risk

Absolute CHD risk <20%
TC ≥5.0 mmol/l
(190 mg/dl)

Lifestyle advice with
the goal of reducing
TC <5.0 mmol/l
(190 mg/dl) and
LDL-C <3.0 mmol/l
(115 mg/dl). Follow-up
at a minimum of 5 years

Absolute CHD risk ≥20%

Measure fasting lipids:
total cholesterol and
HDL-cholesterol,
triglycerides and calculate
LDL-cholesterol**

Lifestyle advice for at
least 3 months with
repeat lipid measurements

TC <5.0 mmol/l
(190 mg/dl) and
LDL-C <3.0 mmol/l
(115 mg/dl).
Maintain lifestyle
advice with annual
follow-up

TC ≥5.0 mmol/l
(190 mg/dl) and/or
LDL-C ≥3.0 mmol/l
(115 mg/dl).
Maintain lifestyle
advice with drug
therapy#

* High CHD risk ≥20% over 10 years or will exceed 20% if
projected to age 60 years

** HDL-cholesterol <1.0 mmol/l (40 mg/dl) and fasting
triglycerides >2.0 mmol/l (180 mg/dl) are markers of increased
coronary risk.

Consider genetically determined hyperlipidaemias (total
cholesterol usually >8.0 mmol/l (above 300 mg/dl) with stigmata
of hyperlipidaemia and a family history of premature CHD) and
causes of secondary hyperlipidaemia such as obesity, diabetes,
alcohol, hypothyroidism, liver and renal diseases. If appropriate
refer to a specialist.

Figure 5.2 **Primary prevention guide to lipid management recommended by the
Joint European Societies** (adapted from Eur Heart J 1998; 19:(10): 1434–1503).

Table 5.8. The latter diet is reserved for specific cholesterol-
lowering in those who fail to achieve satisfactory lipid
reduction with more modest dietary changes.

After a trial of diet for 3 months, the lipid profile should be repeated. In practice, many patients find it difficult to keep to a diet which is effective at lowering cholesterol by more than a few percent. Some patients do, however, show a dramatic response to diet with a substantial fall in cholesterol but this is unusual. If cholesterol is still above threshold values, or the calculation of absolute risk of CHD event does not achieve target values, then drug therapy should be considered.

- Stop smoking

- Increase exercise

- Lose weight if overweight

- NCEP Step 1 diet:
  - Limit alcohol intake to 2 units per day
  - Adjust total calorie intake so as to achieve ideal body weight
  - Increase intake of dietary fibre, particularly soluble fibre
  - Increase intake of complex carbohydrate
  - Reduce total fat to <30% of calories
  - Reduce saturated fat to <10% of calories
  - Encourage fat intake to be in the form of mono- or polyunsaturated fats
  - Reduce dietary cholesterol to <300 mg per day.

- NCEP Step 2 diet:
  - Reduce saturated fat to <7% of total calories
  - Reduce dietary cholesterol to <200 mg per day

Table 5.8 Dietary and lifestyle changes recommended in the management of hyperlipidaemia.

Drug therapy for the treatment of hyperlipidaemia

The major classes of lipid-lowering drugs are shown in Table 5.9. Since their lipid-lowering action works by different mechanisms their effect may be synergistic in combination. The choice of agent will depend in part upon the lipid abnormalities. For example, HMG-CoA reductase inhibitors generally achieve the greatest reduction in LDL-cholesterol and total serum cholesterol, while fibric acid

HMG-CoA reductase inhibitors: 'statins':	Simvastatin
	Pravastatin
	Fluvastatin
	Atorvastatin
	Cerivastatin
Fibric acid derivatives 'fibrates':	Bezafibrate
	Fenofibrate
	Ciprofibrate
Bile sequestering agents 'resins':	Cholestyramine
	Colestipol
Nicotinic acid derivatives:	Acipimox
Fish oils:	Maxepa

HMG – 3-hydroxy 3-methylglutaryl

Table 5.9 **Major groups of lipid-lowering drugs in common usage.**

derivatives have a greater effect in lowering triglycerides but less effect on LDL-cholesterol.

Statins (3-hydroxy 3-methylglutaryl-CoA reductase inhibitors)

These agents inhibit 3-hydroxy 3-methylglutaryl-Co enzyme A (HMG-CoA) reductase, the enzyme controlling the rate-limiting step in cholesterol biosynthesis. These powerful agents can achieve a substantial reduction of 30% to 40% in LDL-cholesterol. They have revolutionised the treatment of hypercholesterolaemia because of their efficacy and safety in large trials, and the newer agents (such as atorvastatin) may even achieve greater reductions.

Recent large studies in both secondary and primary prevention, such as 4S, WOSCOPS, CARE, and the most recently presented Long-term Intervention with Pravastatin in Ischaemic Heart Disease trial (the LIPID study) have all demonstrated a reduction in all-cause mortality in addition to a significant reduction in coronary events following treatment with statins. This was in contrast to the earlier studies using fibrates and bile acid sequestering agents, as there was no excess of non-cardiovascular mortality in the statin treatment groups in the latter studies. The reduction in mortality is unlikely to be class specific, as a similar effect upon cardiovascular mortality and on regression of coronary atheroma is observed with other agents.

The four modern intervention studies have demonstrated the considerable safety and exceptional tolerance of the statins. Patients treated with statins may show a slight elevation of muscle and liver enzymes. A significant elevation of these enzymes (greater than five times the upper limit of normal) or muscle pain may require treatment to be stopped. Rhabdomyolysis has been reported rarely. Sleep disturbance has also been suggested because some of the drugs in this class are able to cross the blood-brain barrier. The more commonly reported adverse effects include fatigue, sleep disturbance, skin rashes, nausea, and muscle aches, with or without biochemical evidence of myopathy. These side-effects lead to discontinuation rates of statin therapy in the region of 6%–12%. Clinical myopathy increases with combination therapy with gemfibrozil, cyclosporin and nicotinic acid. Hepatic transaminaises may rise up to three times the upper limit of normal in 2% of subjects. It is recommended, therefore, that liver enzymes and creatine kinase be measured 6 to 8 weeks after commencement of therapy. Care is needed with the statins as they can potentiate the effects of anticoagulants, and the prothrombin ratio should be re-checked soon after initiating treatment.

Drug group	Effect on serum levels		
	Total cholesterol	HDL-cholesterol	Total fasting triglycerides
Statins	↓20–35%	↑2–10%	↓10–25%
Fibrates	↓10–20%	↑10–25%	↓30–60%
Bile acid resins	↓10–20%	↑1–5%	Little effect
↓decrease, ↑increase			

Table 5.10 Major lipid-lowering therapies: effects on lipids and lipoprotein levels.

Comparisons of reductions in the various lipid and lipoprotein fractions in response to statin or other drug therapies are shown in Table 5.10. Statins are the most powerful agents with regard to reduction of total and LDL-cholesterol, whereas fibrates have a more powerful effect on triglycerides. There are currently five different statins licensed for clinical use (Table 5.9), with costs ranging from £12.95 (100 µg cerivastatin) to £94.08 (80 mg atorvastatin) per month prescription (UK figures). Choice of which statin to prescribe will be made on efficacy data, degree of evidence-based trial data, cost and side-effect profile. Whilst all five statins are extremely well tolerated, cerivastatin and atorvastatin are the most potent, based on daily dose needed to achieve a 30% reduction in LDL-cholesterol (Table 5.11).

	Relative potency	Daily dose (mg)
Fluvastatin	1	60
Pravastatin	1	40
Lovastatin	1.5	40
Simvastatin	6	10
Atorvastatin	12	5
Cerivastatin	300	0.2

Table 5.11 Relative potency of the 'statins' based on a daily dose needed to achieve a 30% reduction in LDL-cholesterol.

On a cost basis, fluvastatin and cerivastatin are significantly less expensive compared to the others, with cerivastatin in addition exhibiting less drug interactions (e.g. with warfarin). However, the evidence-base from cardiovascular outcome trials is with simvastatin, pravastatin and most recently with lovastatin (AFCAPS/TexCAPS Study). The significance of the non-lipid properties of statins which may help to explain the early and significant cardiovascular event reduction in several trials have still to be elucidated.

Whilst cost-effectiveness and, as a result, the absolute level of risk required to initiate treatment, will continue to be debated, this issue will become less controversial over the next 5 years owing to the slow decrease in the costs of statins. Patents will also start to expire early after the Millennium!

Fibrates

The fibrates include clofibrate, gemfibrozil, bezafibrate, fenofibrate, and ciprofibrate. Though the mechanisms of action of the fibrates are complex, they reduce very low-density lipoprotein (VLDL) by a combination of decreased production and increased clearance. There is less free fatty acid flux, associated with less VLDL production and increased activity of the clearance enzyme lipoprotein lipase. The predominant effect is the lowering of triglyceride by about 30%, with an approximate 10% increase in HDL-cholesterol. Although LDL-cholesterol is lowered by fibrates, the reductions achieved by the older fibrates (clofibrate, gemfibrozil and bezafibrate) are between 5% and 15%, whereas the newer fibrates (fenofibrate and ciprofibrate) are more effective with reductions of between 24% and 30%.

Fibrates provoke different responses according to the pattern of hyperlipidaemia. For example, in Type 2B hyperlipidaemia fibrates lower both cholesterol and triglycerides, whereas they exhibit a greater LDL-lowering effect in Type 3 hyperlipidaemia where a marked decrease may be shown in both triglyceride and cholesterol levels.

Fibrates are generally well tolerated. The most commonly reported adverse events include gastrointestinal upset, headache, myalgia, sleep disturbance, skin rashes, and pruritus in 5%–10% of patients. Because of the increase in bowel lithogenicity due to fibrates, the long-term risk of gall-stone formation is increased. Frank hepatitis or myositis is rare, but biochemical abnormalities may occur, including abnormal liver function tests and an increase in creatine kinase. Monitoring of prothrombin time is required for patients on oral anticoagulants, as fibrates may potentiate the action of warfarin. Fibrates may be used particularly effectively in combination with a resin. The combination of a fibrate with a statin, however, carries increased risk of myopathy.

Resins

The resins (cholestyramine and colestipol), which are not systemically absorbed, act by irreversibly binding bile salts in the gastrointestinal lumen by exchanging them for chloride ions. This results in intracellular cholesterol depletion. LDL-cholesterol may be lowered by 10% to 20%, accompanied by a rise in HDL-cholesterol of 10%. Triglyceride levels, however, may rise by as much as 30%.

The major role of resins is in combination therapy – they are no longer a first line therapy in hypercholesterolaemia. They are, however, an effective combination therapy with statins or fibrates. Compliance is a major problem because of poor palatability and adverse gastrointestinal effects. These include bloating, flatulence, constipation and nausea. The absorption of other concomitant drugs may also be impaired. These include digoxin, amiodarone, thyroxine and warfarin. There is also reduced folic acid and fat soluble vitamin absorption, but clinical deficiency states are very rare.

Nicotinic acid compounds

Nicotinic acid reduces cholesterol levels by ≤20% and triglyceride levels by approximately 28%. These changes are due to a decrease in VLDL synthesis. There is also a rise in HDL-cholesterol, particularly in the HDL2 sub-fraction. The other preparations in this group include nicofuranose and the newer acipimox. The most prominent side-effect is cutaneous vasodilatation, which is at a maximum during the first weeks of therapy and may then decline. Other adverse effects include skin rashes, hyperuricaemia, gastrointestinal side-effects, hyperglycaemia (therapy is therefore not usually advised in diabetic patients) and hepatic dysfunction. Acipimox, a nicotinic acid derivative, shows less incidence of flushing.

Fish oils

Fatty acids of the omega 3 series have long been known to lower triglyceride levels by reducing VLDL production. Large reductions in triglyceride levels have been observed in some patients by up to 60%. There is a variable rise in LDL-cholesterol on fish oil therapy. Side effects include dyspepsia and flatulence.

Probucol

Probucol is an agent which has both antioxidant and cholesterol-lowering properties. It causes a modest reduction in LDL-cholesterol of 8% to 17% and reduces HDL, particularly the HDL2 sub-fraction, by 15% to 25%. In spite of its interesting antioxidant properties, and the fact that it has been in use for nearly 20 years, the drug has been little studied in clinical trials. It is generally well tolerated, but has a consistent effect on cardiac conduction, prolonging the QT interval, and so may not be used in patients with disturbances of cardiac rhythm. Gastrointestinal side effects may occur. A clinical role for this agent has therefore not been determined, and it is rarely used.

Drug combinations

When the use of a single drug fails to achieve acceptable lipid levels, the use of combination therapy is indicated. Combination therapy is often necessary in the treatment of the inherited hyperlipidaemias. It is rational to use only those combinations which have an added or synergistic effect, although certain combinations should be avoided because of their potential for side-effects. In more severe or refractory hypercholesterolaemias, resulting from elevations in LDL, treatment with a bile acid-sequestering resin in combination with a fibrate or an HMG-CoA reductase inhibitor may be appropriate. A resin with an HMG-CoA reductase inhibitor probably represents the most effective choice. The use of an HMG-CoA reductase inhibitor and a fibrate, however, may be considered, and the patient monitored for the increased risk of myopathy or rhabdomyolysis.

The Fredricksson classification of the hyperlipidaemias and the numerous different genetic phenotypes determining hyperlipidaemia are complicated, so for practical purposes hyperlipidaemia can be divided into four major types:

Type	LDL-C	TG	Terminology
A	↑	Normal	**Hypercholesterolaemia**
B	Normal	↑	**Hypertriglyceridaemia**
C	↑	↑	**Combined hyperlipidaemia**
D	↑↑	↑↑↑	**Marked combined hyperlipidaemia**

The following two tables (Tables 5.12 and 5.13) outline a typical management plan, including advice concerning when to refer to a local lipid service, exclusion of secondary causes and the important physical signs for each of the four categories.

A good relationship between the general practitioner and the hospital-based lipid clinic is important. The lipid clinic has specialist advice and laboratory facilities available, and can also provide specialist cardiological advice. There is easy access to dietetic services. Patients with familial hypercholesterolaemias or severe forms of hyperlipidaemia should be managed initially and in the long-term by a hospital-based lipid clinic. The rarer genetic forms of hyperlipidaemia should certainly be referred for specialist advice, which may be supra regional. These rarer conditions include:

1. • Primary mixed hyperlipidaemias
   • Type 3 lipoproteinaemia
   • Familial combined hyperlipidaemia

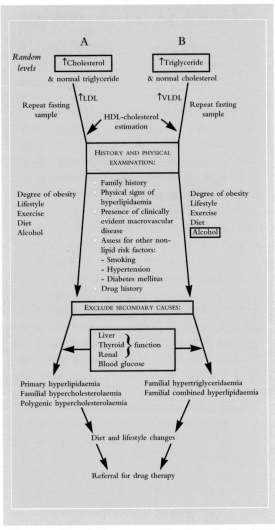

Table 5.12 Guidelines for the management of patients with either isolated hypercholesterolaemia (Type A) or hypertriglyceridaemia (Type B).

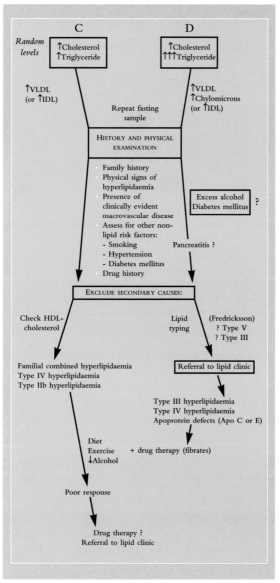

Table 5.13 Guidelines for the management of patients with either mild (Type C) or severe (Type D) combined hyperlipidaemia.

- Hyperapobetalipoproteinaemia
- Familial lecithin cholesterol acyl transferase deficiency
- Fish-eye disease

2. • Primary hypercholesterolaemia
   • Homozygous and heterozygous familial hypercholesterolaemia
   • Familial defective apo B-100
   • Familial hyperalphalipoproteinaemia
   • Cholesterol ester storage disease

Acute severe combined hyperlipidaemia

Special attention is required in the management of acute severe combined hyperlipidaemia of either the primary Type III or V forms, or when associated with pancreatitis, alcoholism, or diabetic ketoacidosis. The major risk with markedly elevated serum triglyceride levels and lipaemia is pancreatitis. Acute or chronic pancreatitis, particularly when associated with alcohol abuse, may present with abdominal pain, lipaemia, diabetes mellitus and gout. The discontinuation of alcohol or normalisation of blood glucose with intravenous insulin will lead to a rapid reversal of lipaemia. Plasmapheresis is rarely needed. Lipaemia associated with diabetic ketoacidosis may be successfully treated with intravenous insulin and fluids alone. Pseudohyponatraemia (an artificially low sodium concentration caused by lipid interference with a photometric sodium assay) associated with lipaemia should also be considered.

Other therapies for refractory hyperlipidaemia

Other therapies may be considered in specialised centres for patients when conventional therapy fails to control hyperlipidaemia or cannot be tolerated by the patient. These methods include extra corporeal removal of lipoproteins, for example by plasma exchange or LDL apheresis, and surgical techniques including partial ileal bypass, portocaval shunt and liver transplantation. Gene therapy is still in the experimental stage.

Disadvantages of the surgical approaches include significant side-effects – ileal bypass may cause diarrhoea and thrombosis of the portocaval shunt, resulting in a failure to lower serum cholesterol. Liver transplantation may represent the most definitive treatment for homozygous familial hypercholesterolaemia, but it is not without risk, including risks of long-term use of immunosuppressive therapy. In a limited number of successful transplants, however, cholesterol-lowering has been dramatic, and has resulted in regression of tendon xanthomata.

Key issues in the management of lipid disorders

Approaches to management of hypercholesterolaemia, specifically because of its relationship to the devastating rate of CHD in the UK, have exercised the medical profession and health policy makers for many years. Serum cholesterol levels are high in the UK with 27% of men and 30% of women having levels above 6.5 mmol/l. As serum cholesterol levels are directly related to macrovascular risk, it is likely that a population-based approach would reduce the incidence of CHD. Estimates suggest that a 10% reduction in plasma cholesterol in the UK population would result in a 27% reduction in overall coronary heart disease mortality.

Results from the recent prospective trials of lipid-lowering drug therapy have shown impressive reduction in CHD rate and in overall mortality. This particularly applies to secondary prevention. In 1993 the British Hyperlipidaemia Association guidelines stated that dietary modifications along with modification of other lifestyle risk factors should be the cornerstone of any CHD prevention strategy. Aggressive drug therapy should be reserved for those at highest risk. These guidelines are shortly to be updated but have a similar theme to the 1993 guidelines. They will continue to define risk not by a number, but by the clinical state, so that the numbers are a guide, but the clinical state (which includes other risk factors) is more important and enables calculation of absolute risk. Emphasis again is placed, as in the European and United States guidelines, on secondary prevention.

Currently, lipid-lowering drugs account for about 2.5% of all prescriptions written in the UK. Statin use, in particular, is rising fast, and statins now make up 1.27% of UK prescriptions. The cost-effectiveness debate continues, particularly for primary prevention. It may be relevant, however, that the earlier statins will be off patent in the next few years – this will have a dramatic effect on the cost-effectiveness issues and arguments! It is clear that targeting high-risk subjects or those who have clinical evidence of macrovascular disease is one approach, but that primary prevention must rely on population initiatives with an appropriate large resource to effectively treat a reducing threshold of absolute CHD risk.

FURTHER READING

Chapter one

1. Ginsberg HN, Le N-A, Gibson JC. Regulation of the production and catabolism of plasma low density lipoprotein in hypertriglyceridaemic subjects. J Clin Invest 1985; 75: 614–23.
2. Eckel RH. Lipoprotein lipase: a multifunctional enzyme relevant to common metabolic diseases. N Engl J Med 1989; 320: 1060–8.
3. Durrington PN. Lipoproteins and their metabolism. In Hyperlipidaemia – Diagnosis and Management. London: Wright; 1989.
4. Goldstein JL, Brown MS. The low density lipoprotein pathway and its relation to atherosclerosis. Ann Rev Biochem 1977; 46: 897–930.
5. Barter PJ. High density lipoproteins and reverse cholesterol transport. Curr Opin Lipidol 1993; 4: 210–17.
6. Packard CJ. Plasma lipid and lipoprotein metabolism in the 1990s – what we know and what we need to know. In Lipids: Current Perspectives: 1 (Chapter 1): 1–20.
7. Bain SC. Lipoprotein metabolism. In: Lipids, Diabetes and Vascular Disease 2nd Ed. Ed. Dobson PM, Barnett AH. Chapter 2: 15–22. Science Press Limited; 1998.
8. Brown MS, Goldstein JL. Receptor mediated endocytosis: insights from the lipoprotein receptor system. Proc Natl Acad Sci USA 1979; 76: 3330–7.
9. Utermann G. Apolipoprotein E polymorphisms in health and disease. Am Heart J 1987; 113: 433–40.
10. Foster DM, Chait A, Albers JJ et al. Evidence for kinetic heterogenicity among low density lipoproteins. Metab Clin Exp 1986; 35: 685–96.

Chapter two

1. Ross R. The pathogenesis of atherosclerosis – an update. N Engl J Med 1998; 314: 488–500.

6

2. Stout LC, Thorpe LW. Histology of normal aortas in non-human primates with emphasis on diffuse intimal thickening. Atherosclerosis 1980; 35: 165–180.

3. Steinberg D, Pathasarathy S, Carew TE et al. Beyond cholesterol: modification of low density lipoprotein that increases its atherogenicity. N Engl J Med 1989; 320: 915–924.

4. Gordon T, Castelli WP, Hjortland MC, Kannel WB, Dawber TR. High density lipoprotein as a protective factor against coronary heart disease – the Framingham Study. Am J Med 1997; 62: 707-14.

5. Pocock SJ, Shaper AG, Phillips AN. Concentrations of high density lipoprotein cholesterol, triglycerides and total cholesterol in ischaemic heart disease. Br Med J 1989; 298: 998–1002.

6. Castelli WP. Epidemiology of triglycerides: a view from Framingham. Am J Cardiol 1992; 70: 3H–9H.

7. Gunby P. Cardiovascular diseases remain Nation's leading cause of death. JAMA 1992; 267: 335–6.

8. Miller NE, Hammet F, Saltissi S et al. Relation of angiographically defined coronary artery disease to plasma lipoprotein subfractions and apolipoproteins. Br Med J 1981; 1: 1741–4.

9. Mann JI, Lewis B, Shepherd J et al. Blood lipid concentrations and other cardiovascular risk factors: distribution, prevalence and detection in Britain. Br Med J 1988; 296: 1702–6.

10. Bhatnagar D, Anand IS, Durrington PN et al. Coronary risk factors in people from the Indian Sub-Continent living in West London and their siblings in India. Lancet 1995; 345: 405–9.

11. Keys A. Seven Countries. A multivariate analysis of death and coronary heart disease. Harvard University Press; 1980.

Chapter three

1. Martin MJ, Hulley SB, Browner WS, Kuller LH, Wentworth D. Serum cholesterol, blood pressure and mortality: implications from a cohort of 361,662 men. Lancet 1986; 2 (8513): 933–6.

2. Thelle DS, Shaper AG, Whitehead TP et al. Blood lipids in middle-aged British men. Br Heart J 1983; 49: 205–13.

3. British Hyperlipidaemia Association: Detection and management of blood lipid disorders. London: Current Science; 1990.

4. Expert panel on the detection, evaluation and treatment of high blood cholesterol in adults. Summary of the second report of the National Cholesterol Education Programme (NCEP) Expert Panel on detection, evaluation and treatment of high blood cholesterol in adults (Adult Treatment Panel II). J Am Med Assoc 1993; 269: 3015–23.

5. Recommendations of the European Atherosclerosis Society prepared by the International Task Force for Prevention of Coronary Heart Disease. Prevention of Coronary Heart Disease: scientific background and new clinical guidelines. Nutrit Metabol Cardiovas Dis 1992; 2 (3): 113–56.

6. Durrington PN. Classification of hyperlipoproteinaemia. In: Hyperlipidaemia – Diagnosis and Management. Chapter 4: 87–90. London: Wright; 1989.

7. Feher MD, Richmond W. In: Lipids and Lipid Disorders. London: Wolfe; 1991.

8. Thompson GR. In: A Handbook of Hyperlipidaemia. London: Current Science Limited; 1989.

9. Pyorala K, De Backer G, Graham I, Poole-Wilson P, Wood D, on behalf of the Task Force. Prevention of coronary heart disease in clinical practice: recommendations of the Task Force of the European Atherosclerosis Society and European Society of Hypertension. Eur Heart J 1994; 15: 1300–31.

10. Winder AF, Dodson PM, Galton DJ. Opthalmological complications of the hyperlipidaemias. Trans Ophthalmol Soc (UK) 1980; 100 (1): 119–22.

Chapter four

1. Law MR, Wald NJ, Thompson SG. By how much and how quickly does reduction in serum cholesterol concentration lower risk of ischaemic heart disease. Br Med J 1994; 308: 367–72.

2. Rossow JE. Lipid-lowering interventions in angiographic trials. Am J Cardiol 1995; 76: 86C–92C.

3. Scandinavian Simvastatin Survival Study Group. Randomised trial of cholesterol-lowering in 4444 patients with coronary heart disease: the Scandinavian Simvastatin Survival Study (4 'S'). Lancet 1994; 344: 1383–9.

4. Lipid Research Clinics Program: The lipid research clinics coronary primary prevention trial results: I. Reduction in incidence of coronary heart disease. JAMA 1984; 251: 351–64.

5. Frick MH, Elo O, Haapa K et al. Helsinki Heart Study: primary prevention trial with gemfibrozil in middle-aged men with dyslipidaemia. N Engl J Med 1987; 317: 1237–45.

6. Shepherd J, Cobbe SM, Ford I et al. Prevention of coronary heart disease with pravastatin in men with hypercholesterolaemia. N Engl J Med 1995; 333: 1301–7.

7. Sacks FM, Pfeffer MA, Moye LA et al. The effect of pravastatin on coronary events after myocardial infarction in patient with average cholesterol levels. N Engl J Med 1996; 335: 1001–9.

8. Downs JR, Clearfield M, Weis S et al. Primary prevention of Acute Coronary Events with lovastatin in men and women with average cholesterol levels. Results of AFCAPS/TexCAPS. JAMA 1998; 279: 1615–1622.

Chapter five

1. Department of Health. The Health of the Nation: what you can do about it. London: Department of Health Information Pack; 1995.

2. Reckless JPD. The economics of cholesterol lowering. Baillieres Clin Endocrinol Metabol 1990; 4: 947–72.

3. Pharoah PDP, Hollingworth W. Cost-effectiveness of lowering cholesterol concentration with statins in patients with and without pre-existing coronary heart disease. Br Med J 1996; 312: 1443–8.

4. Expert panel on the detection, evaluation and treatment of high blood cholesterol in adults (adult treatment panel II). Summary of the second report of the National Cholesterol Education Programme (NCEP). J Am Med Assoc 1993; 269: 3015–23.

5. Pyorala K, De Backer G, Graham I, Poole-Wilson P, Wood D, on behalf of the Task Force. Prevention of coronary heart disease in clinical practice: recommendations of the Task Force of the European Atherosclerosis Society and European Society of Hypertension. Eur Heart J 1994; 15: 1300–31.

6. Betteridge DJ, Dodson PM, Durrington PN et al. Management of hyperlipidaemia: guidelines of he British Hyperlipidaemia Association. Postgrad Med J 1993; 69: 359–69.

7. American College of Physicians. Guidelines for using serum cholesterol, high density lipoprotein cholesterol and triglyceride levels as screening tests for preventing heart disease in adults. Ann Intern Med 1996; 124: 515–17.

8. Winyard G. SMAC statement on the use of statins. London: Department of Health; 1997.

9. Ramsay LE, Haq IV, Jackson PR, Yeo WW, Pickin DM, Payne JN. Targeting lipid-lowering drug therapy for primary prevention of coronary disease: an updated Sheffield table. Lancet 1996; 348: 377–8.

10. Dodson PM, Bayly G. Soluble Fibre and Cholesterol Reduction. Kent: Publishing Initiatives; 1997.

11. Illingworth DR, Erkelens DW, Keller et al. Defined daily doses in relation to hypolipidaemic efficacy of lovastatin, pravastatin and simvastatin. Lancet 1994; 343: 1554–5.

12. Larsen ML, Illingworth DR. Triglyceride-lowering agents: fibrates and nicotinic acid. Curr Opin Lipidol 1993; 4: 34–40.

13. Levine GN, Keaney JF, Vita JA. Cholesterol reduction in cardiovascular disease, clinical benefits and possible mechanisms. N Engl J Med 1995; 332: 512–21.

14. Jones AF, Dodson PM. Management of dyslipidaemia in diabetes mellitus. In Lipids, Diabetes and Vascular Disease, 2nd Ed. Eds. Dodson PM, Barnett AH. London: Science Press Ltd; 1998.

15. Stein E, Sprecher D, Allenby KS et al. Cerivastatin, a new potent synthetic HMG-CoA reductase inhibitor. J Cardiovasc Pharmacol Ther 1997; 2: 7–16.
16. Rosenow RS, Tangney CC. Antiatherothrombotic properties of statins. Implications for cardiovascular event reduction. JAMA 1998; 279: 1643–1650.
17. Second Joint Task Force of European and other Societies on Coronary Prevention. Prevention of coronary heart disease in clinical practice. Eur Heart J 1998; 19 (10): 1434–1503.
18. Wood D, Durrington P, Poulter, N, McInnes G, Rees A, Wray R. Joint British recommendations on prevention of coronary heart disease in clinical practice. Heart 1998; 80 (Suppl 2): S1–S29.

INDEX

Page numbers in bold indicate a figure or table.

A

ACAT, 9
ACE inhibitors, 35, 36
acute severe combined hyperlipidaemia, 62
AFCAPS/TexCAPS, 35
age, as a risk factor, 15, 17
alcohol, as a risk factor, 24, 46, 50, 60
American College of Physicians advocations, 38
angina, 12, 42
apolipoproteins, 2–7
    A, 6
    B, 4–5, 7, 11
    C, 6–7; Apo C-II deficiency, 23
    defects, physical signs of, 25–6
    E, 4–7, 22; homozygosity, 22–3; polymorphisms, 5;
        receptor, 5–7, **8**
arteriole intima, thickening of, 10
aspirin, 36
atherosclerosis, 7, 10–14, 28
    arteriole intima, thickening of, 10
    atheroma formation, 10–14; common sites, 11
    calcification, 11
    collagen, 11
    corneal arcus, 25
    elastin, 11
    endothelial cell injury hypothesis, 11
    fatty streaks, 10
    fibrous plaques, 10–11
    foam cells, 10–12; proliferation, 11–12
    macrophages, 10–12; growth factors, 12
    necrotic cells, 10
    treating lipid disorders to reduce, 29–30
artery, 10

7

B

beta-blockers, 24, 46
bile salts, 5, 9, 57
bile sequestering agents, *see* resins
British Hyperlipidaemia Association guidelines for management, 63
British Hyperlipidaemia Association guidelines for treatment, 41
British Regional Heart Survey, 29
bypass grafting surgery, 13, 34

C

calcification, 11
cardiac failure, 12
CARE, 32–4, 48
CHD, *see* coronary heart disease
cholesterol, 1, 3–6, 8–10, 14–16, 20, 21–3, 37–8, 43–4, 54
    and coronary heart disease, 15–16, 20–1, 29–30
    emulsification, 5
    esters, 1, 5–6, 9–10
    excretion, *see* reverse cholesterol transport
    HDL-cholesterol, 15, 17, 21, 33, 40, 44, 54, 55
    LDL-cholesterol, 4, 11, 14–16, 22, 25, 29, 32–3, 40–41, 54, 55
    reverse transport, 5, 8, **8**, 17
    synthesis, 5–6
    target levels, 32–5, 42–3, 47, **48**
Cholesterol and Recurrent Events trial, *see* CARE
cholestyramine, 31
chylomicrons, 3–6, 8, 22
    remnants, *see* IDL
circulation
    enterohepatic, 9
    of lipids, 2–5
classification of hyperlipidaemia, 21–4, 56
collagen, 11
combinations of drugs, 54, 57, 58
combined hyperlipidaemia, 20–3
Combined Task Force of the European Societies coronary risk chart, **18**, 41
computerised risk assessment, 45
corneal arcus, 25, **25**

Coronary Drug Project, 33
coronary heart disease (CHD)
    and cholesterol, 14–16, 20–1, 29–30
    economic costs, 13–14, 41–2, 64
    and HDL, 16–17, 30
    lipid risk factors, 10–19
    mortality, 12–14, **14**, 16, 29, 31, 33, 53, 63
    non-lipid risk factors, 17–19
    population risk, 14–17, 29–36
    risk factors (general), 14–15; absolute risk, 41, 47, **48**, 49;
        calculation of coronary risk, 18–19; categories of those at
        risk, 37–8; Combined Task Force of the European
        Societies coronary risk chart, **18**, 41
    screening, 38–43; lipid measurement, 40–41; population, 38,
        63; risk assessment, 41–5; subjects, 39–40; targeted, 39
    treatment, 29–30; intervention trials, 31–5
    and triglycerides, 15–17
cost-effectiveness, of lipid-lowering, 36, 41–2, 55, 64
cyclosporin, 54

D

diabetes mellitus, 15, 17–19, 24, 42, 43, 44, 45, 46
diagnosis, of hyperlipidaemia, 46–7
diet, 31, 34, 52, 63
    LA Veterans Study, 33
drugs
    combinations, 54, 57, 58
    intervention trials, 31–6
    therapy, 47, 52–3; ACE inhibitors, 36, aspirin, 36, fibrates,
        31, 33, 53, 56–7; fish oils, 53, 58; niacin, 33; nicotinic acid
        compounds, 31, 33, 53, 57; probucol, 58; resins, 31, 57;
        statins, 31, 34, 35, 42, 52, 53–6, 64; warfarin, 35, 56
    trials, 31–6; CARE, 32–3, 53; Coronary Drug Project, 33;
        Helsinki Heart Study, 33; LA Veterans Study, 33; LIPID
        Study, 33, 34, 53; LRC-CCP Trial, 33; MRFIT Study,
        15–16, **15**, 29; POSCH Study, 31; 4S, 32–3, 53;
        Stockholm Study, 33; WHO Co-operative Trial, 33;
        WOSCOPS, 32–3, 34, 37, 43, 53.

E

elastin, 11
endogenous pathway, 6–7, **7**

endothelial cell injury hypothesis, 11
enterohepatic circulation, 9
European Atherosclerosis Society guidelines, 21, **48**
excretion, of cholesterol, 8–9
exercise, 50, 52
exogenous pathway, 5–6, **6**

F

familial combined hyperlipidaemia, 23, 37
familial hypercholesterolaemia, 22–3, 44
family history, 15, 17, 42, 46, 47
family screening, 39
fatty acids, 1–2, 5–6, 56
fatty streaks, 10
fibrates, 31, 33, 53, 56–7
    adverse effects, 57
    bezafibrate, 53, 56
    ciprofibrate, 53, 56
    clofibrate, 33, 50; WHO Co-operative Trial, 33; Stockholm
        Study, 33
    combination therapy, 58
    fenofibrate, 53, 56
    gemfibrozil, 33, 53, 56; Helsinki Heart Study, 33
fibric acid derivatives, *see* fibrates
fibrinogen, 7
fibrous plaques, 10–11
fish oils, 58
    adverse effects, 58
    Maxepa, 53
foam cells, 10–12
    proliferation, 11–12
Framingham Heart Study, 16–17, **16, 17**, 40
Fredricksson classification of hyperlipidaemia, 21–3, **22**, 59
Friedewald formula, 40

G

genetics, as a risk factor, 15
glycerol, 2, **2**, 6
guidelines
    American College of Physicians, 38
    British Hyperlipidaemia Associaton, 41, 63
    European Atherosclerosis Society, 21, 48

Hypercholesterolaemia, management, 60
Hypertriglyceridaemia, management, 60
Joint British Recommendations on Prevention of Coronary Heart Disease in Clinical Practice, 45, 48,49
Joint European Recommendations on Prevention of Coronary Heart Disease in Clinical Practice, 49, 51
National Cholesterol Education Programme (NCEP), 37, 38, 41, 50
Standing Medical Advisory Committee (SMAC), 43, 44

H

HDL, 3–4, 6–8, 16–17, 23, 40
    and coronary heart disease, 16–17, 30
    reverse cholesterol transport 5, 8, **8**, 17
    subfractions, 4, 57
HDL-cholesterol, 15, 17, 21, 33, 40, 44, 56, 57
Helsinki Heart Study, 33
hepatosplenomegaly, 27
high density lipoprotein, *see* HDL
HMG-CoA reductase, 8–9
    inhibitors, *see* statins
    synthesis, 8–9
hyperalphalipoproteinaemia, 23, 62
hyperapobetalipoproteinaemia, 62
hypercholesterolaemia, 20–3, 25, 28, 57
    familial, 22–3
    guidelines for management, 60
hyperlipidaemia, 20–8
    acute severe combined hyperlipidaemia, 62
    classification, 20–4; primary hyperlipidaemias, 20, 22–3, **23**; secondary hyperlipidaemias, 20, 22, 24
    clinical features, 24, **26**; corneal arcus, 25, **25**; hepatosplenomegaly, 27; lipaemia retinalis, 26–7, 44; pancreatitis, 27, 62; xanthelasma, **24**, 25–6, 44, 45; xanthomata, 25–7, **26**, **27**, 44, 63
    combined hyperlipidaemia, 20–3
    diagnosis, 46–7
    drug therapy, 47, 52–3, 54; ACE inhibitors, 36; aspirin, 36; combinations, 54, 57, 58; fibrates, 31, 33, 55, 56–7; fish oils, 53, 58; niacin, 33; nicotinic acid compounds, 31, 33, 53, 57; probucol, 58; resins, 31, 33, 57; statins, 31, 34, 35, 42, 52, 55–6, 64; warfarin, 35, 56
    Fredricksson classification of hyperlipidaemia, 21–3, **22**, 59

lipid levels, 20–1; screening, 38–45

management, 29–30; 47–64

primary hyperlipidaemias, 20, 22–3, **23**; inheritance of, 22–3

terminology, 20

hypertension, 15, 17–18, 42, 43, 44, 45

hypertriglyceridaemia, 20–3, 27–8, 30

guidelines for management, 60

hypothyroidism, 25

I

IDL, 3, 7–8, 22–3

receptor, 8

inheritance of primary hyperlipidaemias, 22–3

insulin resistance, 17–19

intermediate density lipoprotein, *see* IDL

ischaemic heart disease, 24

ischaemic optic neuropathy, 28

J

Joint British Recommendations on Prevention of Coronary Heart
Disease in Clinical Practice, 45, 48, 49

Joint European Guidelines for the Prevention of Coronary Heart
Disease in Clinical Practice, 49, 51

L

LA Veterans Study, 33

LDL, 3–5, 7–9, 11–12, 22–3

hydrolysis, 8–9, **9**

oxidation, 11–12

receptor, 4–5; 7–9, 22–3; synthesis, 8–9

LDL-cholesterol, 4, 11, 14–16, 22, 24–5, 29, 32–3, 40–41, 56, 57

Friedewald formula, 40

subfractions, 4

lipid clinics, 59

LIPID Study, 33, 34, 53

lipids

circulation, 2–5

fatty streaks, 10

levels, 20–1, 25; EAS guidelines, 21, **48**; Fredricksson
classification, 21–3, 59

lowering, 29–36; drug therapies, 47, 52–53; Joint British

Recommendations on Prevention of Coronary Heart Disease in Clinical Practice, 48; Joint European Guidelines for the Prevention of Coronary Heart Disease in Clinical Practice, 49; Standing Medical Advisory Committee (SMAC) priorities for lipid-lowering, 43, **43**

measurement, 40–41

metabolism, 5–9; endogenous pathway, 6–7, **7**; enterohepatic circulation, 9; exogenous pathway, 5–6, **6**; LDL receptor, 4–5, 7–9, 22–3; reverse cholesterol transport, 5, 8, **8**, 17

risk factors, 10–19

structure, 1–2

lipoproteins, 2–5, 8, 14, 25

apolipoproteins, 2–4

classification, 3–4

HDL, 3–4, 6–8, 16–17, 23, 40; coronary heart disease, 16–17, 30; subfractions, 4, 55

IDL, 3, 7–8, 22–3; receptor, 8

LDL, 3–5, 7–9, 11, 22–3; receptor, 4–5, 7–9, 22–3; LDL-cholesterol, 4, 11, 14–16, 22, 24–5, 29, 32–3, 40–1, 54, 55

lipase, 5–7, 56; deficiency, 23

lipoprotein (a), 7

separation, 3

structure, 2–3; **3**

VLDL, 3–4, 7–8, 22–3, 56, 57

lipoprotein lipase, 5–7, 56

deficiency, 23

liver disease, 24–5, 46

liver transplantation, 63

low density lipoprotein, *see* LDL

LRC-CCP Trial, 33

M

macrophages, 10–12; growth factors, 12

management, of hyperlipidaemia, 23, 29–30; 47–64

acute severe combined hyperlipidaemia, 62

British Hyperlipidaemia Association Guidelines, 63

diagnosis, 46–7

drug therapy, 47, 52–64; ACE inhibitors, 36; aspirin, 36; combinations, 54, 57, 58; fibrates, 31, 33, 54, 56–7; fish oils, 58; niacin, 33; nicotinic acid compounds, 31, 33, 53, 57; probucol, 58; resins, 31, 33, 57; statins, 31, 34, 35, 42, 52, 53–6, 64; warfarin, 35

  key issues, 63–64
  hypercholesterolaemia, 54
  hypertriglyceridaemia, 54
  non-pharmacological management, 46–7
  screening, 37–42; lipid measurement, 39–40; population, 37,
      57; risk assessment, 40–3; subjects, 38–9; targeted, 38
  strategies, 53–6
Metabolic Syndrome, *see* Syndrome X
microvascular disease, 28
      ischaemic optic neuropathy, 28
      retinal artery occlusion, 28, **28**
      retinal vein occlusion, 28, **28**
MRFIT study, 15–16, **15**, 29
myocardial infarction, 13, 31, 32, 34, 35, 42, 43

N

National Cholesterol Education Programme (NCEP) guidelines, 37,
      38, 41, 50, **52**
      Step-1 diet, 50–1, **52**
      Step-2 diet, 50–1, **52**
necrotic cells, 10
nephrotic syndrome, 25
niacin, 33; Coronary Drug Project, 33
nicotinic acid compounds, 31, 33, 54, 57
      acipimox, 57
      adverse effects, 54, 57
      nicofuranose, 57
      nicotinic acid, 57; Stockholm Study, 33

O

obesity, 15, 17–18, 24
opportunistic screening, 39
oral contraceptives, 24

P

pancreatitis, 27, 29, 62
phospholipids, 1–2, 6, 10
physical activity, 15
population screening, 38
      National Cholesterol Education Programme Guidelines, 37
population studies, 14–17

POSCH trial, 31
primary hyperlipidaemias, 20, 22–3, **23**
    Apo C-II deficiency, 23
    Apo E-2 homozygosity, 22–3
    familial combined hyperlipidaemia, 23, 40, 46
    familial hypercholesterolaemia, 22–3, 44
    familial hypertriglyceridaemia, 23
    hyperalphalipoproteinaemia, 23, 39
    inheritance of, 22–3
    lipoprotein lipase deficiency, 23
    polygenic hypercholesterolaemia, 23
probucol, 58
    adverse effects, 58
Procam Study, 41
proteinuria, 44–5

R

renal disease, 24, 46
resins, 31, 57
    adverse effects, 57
    cholestyramine, 31, 33, 53, 57; LRC-CCP Trial, 33
    colestipol, 48, 53, 57
    combination therapy, 58
retinal artery occlusion, 28, **28**
retinal vein occlusion, 28, **28**
reverse transport, of cholesterol, 5, 8, **8**, 17
risk factors for coronary heart disease, 14–15
    absolute risk, 41, 45, 49
    calculation of coronary risk, 18–19
    Combined Task Force coronary risk chart, **18**, 41
    lipid risk factors, 10–19
    non-lipid risk factors, 14, 17–19
    risk assessment, 41–5
    Syndrome X, 17–18, 24

S

4S, 32–3, 53
Scandinavian Simvastatin Survival Study, *see* 4S
screening, 38–45
    family, 39
    lipid measurement, 40–41
    opportunistic, 39

population, 38
risk assessment, 41–5
selective, 39
subjects, 39–40
targeted, 39
secondary hyperlipidaemias, 20, 22, 24
selective screening, 39
Seven Counties Study, 15
sex, as a risk factor, 15, 17
smoking, 15, 17–18, 42, 43, 44, 45, 46, 50
Standing Medical Advisory Committee (SMAC) priorities for lipid-lowering, 43, **43**, 44, **44**
statins, 31, 34, 35–6, 53–6, 64
adverse effects, 54
atorvastatin, 53, 55
cerivastatin, 53, 55
combination therapy, 58
fluvastatin, 53, 55
lovastatin, 35, 55
pravastatin, 34–5, 53, 55; CARE Study, 32–4, 53; LIPID Study, 34, 53; WOSCOPS, 34, 35, 37, 53
simvastatin, 53, 55; 4S, 32–3, 53
steroids, 24
Stockholm Study, 33
structure, of lipids, 1–2
surgery, 62–3
bypass grafting surgery, 13, 34, 62
liver transplantation, 62–3

T

Syndrome X, 17–18, **18**, 24
targeted screening, 39
thiazide diuretics, 24, 46
thrombosis, 7
thyroid disease, 24, 46
treatment, 29–30; 47–64
British Hyperlipidaemia Association Guidelines, 41
trials, 31–6; CARE, 32–4, 53; Coronary Drug Project, 33; Helsinki Heart Study, 33; LA Veterans Study, 33; LIPID Study, 34, 53, 48; LRC-CCP Trial, 33; MRFIT Study, 15–16, **15**, 29; POSCH Study, 31; 4S, 32–3, 53; Stockholm Study, 33; WHO Co-operative Trial, 33;

WOSCOPS, 34, 35, 37, 53
triglycerides, 1–6, **2**, 15–17, 21–3, 27, 40, 54, 56
    and coronary heart disease, 15–17, 30, 32
    emulsification, 5

U

ultracentrifugation, 3

V

very low density lipoprotein, *see* VLDL
VLDL, 3–4, 7–8, 22–3, 56, 57, 58

W

warfarin, 35
West of Scotland Coronary Prevention Study, *see* WOSCOPS.
WHO Co-operative Trial, 33
WOSCOPS, 32–3, 34, 35, 37, 53

X

xanthelasma, **24**, 25–6, 46, 47
xanthomata, 25–7, **26**, **27,** 46, 43